Stress
and
Job
Performance

Advanced Topics in Organizational Behavior

The **Advanced Topics in Organizational Behavior** series examines current and emerging issues in the field of organizational behavior. Written by researchers who are widely acknowledged subject area experts, the books provide an authoritative, up-to-date review of the conceptual, research, and practical implications of the major issues in organizational behavior.

Stress
and
Job
Performance

Theory, Research, and Implications
for Managerial Practice

Steve M. Jex

Advanced Topics in
Organizational Behavior

SAGE Publications
International Educational and Professional Publisher
Thousand Oaks   London   New Delhi

For information:

SAGE Publications, Inc.
2455 Teller Road
Thousand Oaks, California 91320
E-mail: order@sagepub.com

SAGE Publications Ltd.
6 Bonhill Street
London EC2A 4PU
United Kingdom

SAGE Publications India Pvt. Ltd.
M-32 Market
Greater Kailash I
New Delhi 110 048 India

Printed in the United States of America

Library of Congress Cataloging-in-Publication Data

Jex, Steve M.
  Stress and job performance: Theory, research, and implications
for managerial practice / by Steve M. Jex.
    p. cm. – (Advanced topics in organizational behavior)
  Includes bibliographical references and index.

  ISBN 0-7619-0923-0 (cloth: acid-free paper)
  ISBN 0-7619-0924-9 (pbk.: acid-free paper)
  1. Job stress. 2. Labor productivity. I. Title. II. Series.
  HF5548.85 .J49 1998
  158.7—ddc21   98-25435

98 99 00 01 02 03 10 9 8 7 6 5 4 3 2 1

Acquiring Editor:	Marquita Flemming
Editorial Assistant:	MaryAnn Vail
Production Editor:	Diana E. Axelsen
Editorial Assistant:	Denise Santoyo
Typesetter/Designer:	Rose Tylak
Indexer:	Mary Mortensen

Contents

Introduction

O ccupational stress is a topic that has generated a tremendous volume of scholarly research in a relatively short period of time. The reason for such interest, I believe, is that stress in the workplace can have a tremendously negative impact on the functioning of organizations. In fact, many authors have illustrated this by citing an estimate of the amount of money that stress is extracting from the economy (e.g., Aldred, 1994; Ivancevich & Matteson, 1980; Jex & Beehr, 1991; Matteson & Ivancevich, 1987; Mulcahy, 1991). Such estimates are typically based on the assumption that workplace stress leads to increased health care costs, higher rates of absenteeism and turnover, more accidents, and lower levels of performance. Although there is considerable variation, these estimates tend to be in the billions of dollars, thus highlighting the critical economic impact of stress. Stress is also important because organizations have a moral, and increasingly legal, obligation to provide a work environment in which stress is kept to manageable levels.

This book is focused on one small but extremely important part of the occupational stress literature: the relationship between stress and job performance. Although there have certainly been occupational stress studies examining job performance (many of which will be summarized in this book) and even reviews of this area (e.g., Sullivan & Bhagat, 1992), there have been few attempts to provide a comprehensive treatment. This may seem a bit surprising, given the importance of job performance to both occupational stress researchers and managers. For example, in a recent survey conducted by Northwestern National Life Insurance Company, 69% of respondents indicated that high stress reduced their job performance (Mulcahy, 1991).

Why has job performance been neglected in occupational stress research? One primary reason, as will be seen, is that job performance is a very complex variable. As a result, the processes by which stressful job conditions affect job performance are probably also quite complex. At a more practical level, it is very difficult to measure performance accurately. Another, more subtle, reason is that occupational stress researchers have tended to focus on outcomes that have the greatest direct impact on the functioning of individual employees (e.g., depressed mood, health problems, substance abuse). Of these outcomes, health has perhaps received the greatest attention (e.g., Ganster & Schaubroeck, 1991b; Matteson & Ivancevich, 1987).

Unfortunately, compared to outcomes such as mental and physical health, occupational stress researchers have devoted far less attention to outcomes that have a more direct effect on organizations (e.g., job performance). The irony of this neglect is that, for most people, job performance has a high degree of personal relevance. For example, lower levels of job performance may lead to lower levels of self-confidence and self-esteem (Bandura, 1997; Brockner, 1988). Furthermore, to the extent that job stressors depress job performance and ultimately organizational productivity, this may indirectly lead to events that have a tremendously negative impact on individual employees (i.e., layoffs, work overload). This, of course, is not meant to dismiss important outcomes such as mental and physical health. Rather, the point is that other important outcomes, such as job performance, should not be ignored.

In writing this book, I have tried to appeal to a broad audience. As Matteson and Ivancevich (1987) pointed out, most comprehensive treatments of occupational stress have been aimed either *exclusively* at an academic audience (e.g., occupational stress researchers) or *exclusively* at the general public. Although there are pros and cons to each approach, it would be ideal to appeal to *both* types of readers because occupational stress is a topic that is of interest and importance to both. My goal, therefore, is to provide the reader with a rigorous, research-based examination of the relationship between occupational stress and job performance. At the same time, I have tried to use a writing style that is not overly technical in order to make the book understandable and useful to those readers who do not have an extensive background in the behavioral sciences.

The book is organized into six chapters. In Chapter 1, a concise overview of occupational stress is provided to prepare the reader for the chapters that follow.

This includes a brief history of the study of occupational stress, definitions of important terms, and a summary of relevant theoretical models of the stress process. In Chapter 2, major stressors in the workplace are examined. As many readers will note, there are probably an infinite number of things that may make a particular organization stressful. Those covered in the chapter are simply the ones that have received some research attention. Chapter 3 examines job performance as an outcome variable. This major objective of this chapter is to give the reader a feel for the complexity of job performance. Chapter 4 examines empirical evidence on the major question examined in this book: What is the relationship between occupational stress and job performance? In Chapter 5, a number of variables are examined that may affect the relationship between occupational stress and job performance. Finally, in Chapter 6, several issues that need to be considered in future investigations of occupational stress and job performance are discussed.

Acknowledgments

This book would not have been possible without the effort and support of many people. I would first like to thank Julian Barling and Kevin Kelloway for suggesting that a book focusing on occupational stress and job performance was a worthwhile endeavor. I would also like to thank Peter Chen and Gary Adams for reading drafts of the manuscript and making some very valuable suggestions. Their efforts greatly improved the quality of this book. The advice and support of my good friend and mentor Paul Spector were also instrumental in completing this project.

Several students also made valuable contributions to this book. I am especially grateful to Daniel Bachrach for conducting most of the literature searches and helping to keep me on track. Deb Bohlman and Milla Kokotovich also provided very valuable assistance by checking the numerous citations, producing the figures, and generally helping to keep me organized. I also greatly appreciate the support and encouragement of all the I/O psychology graduate students at the University of Wisconsin–Oshkosh.

On a more personal note, I would like to express sincere thanks to my family. My wife, Robin, has been a constant source of love and encouragement throughout my career. Her contributions are embedded in every page of this book. My two young sons, Garrett and Travis, also contributed greatly, although neither of them read a word of the manuscript or have the faintest idea of what this book is about! Their contribution is unconditional love for their dad. The feeling is definitely mutual.

1

An Introduction to Occupational Stress

Compared to other fields of scientific inquiry, the study of occupational stress is relatively new. In fact, the earliest work related to stress can be traced back to the pioneering work of the physiologist Walter Cannon in the early part of this century (Cannon, 1914) and his investigations of the relationship between emotions and physiological responses. The actual scientific investigation of stress goes back only 50 years to the work of Hans Selye (1956), who is generally regarded as the "Father of Stress." The first major program of research investigating stress in organizations was undertaken at the University of Michigan's Institute for Social Research in the early 1960s. This research program produced several widely cited occupational stress studies (e.g., Caplan, Cobb, French, Harrison, & Pinneau, 1975; Kahn, Wolfe, Quinn, Snoek, & Rosenthal, 1964) and served as the training ground for several influential scholars in this field.

Despite the flurry of activity from the Michigan research program, occupational stress was still not a major research area in the organizational sciences in the late 1960s to mid-1970s. This changed in 1978, in large part as a result of Terry Beehr and John Newman's comprehensive review and analysis of the occupational stress literature, published in the journal *Personnel Psychology*. While the Beehr and Newman article is generally regarded as an important scholarly work, perhaps its greatest contribution was to alert those in the organizational sciences that occupational stress was an issue worthy of research attention.

Since the publication of the Beehr and Newman review, the volume of occupational stress research has grown tremendously. In fact, it has grown so much in the past 20 years that several books and chapters have been written summarizing this literature (e.g., Beehr, 1995; Beehr & Bhagat, 1985; Ivancevich & Matteson, 1980; Jex & Beehr, 1991; Kahn & Byosiere, 1992). Given this tremendous increase in research activity, it is clear that much progress has been made toward understanding occupational stress. Unfortunately, however, our understanding of occupational stress is still rather limited, due largely to the complexity of the phenomenon under study and also due to the fact that, despite vast improvements over the years, much occupational stress research still suffers from serious methodological limitations (e.g., Beehr, 1995; Jex & Beehr, 1991; Spector, 1992).

Occupational Stress Terminology

Like any field of study, occupational stress has a unique set of terms that are used to define important variables and concepts. Let's start with the word *stress*. The word stress is derived from the Latin word *strictus*, which means "to tighten." This is appropriate when one thinks of the feelings that often accompany stressful situations. When used in occupational stress research, the word stress can be defined in one of three ways. A *stimulus* definition implies that stress refers to those stimuli in the environment that may require some adaptive response on the part of an employee (i.e., "John has a lot of stress in his job lately"). In contrast, a *response* definition implies that stress refers to the feelings that one experiences when the demands of the job exceed one's ability to cope (i.e., "John is feeling a lot of stress lately because of deadlines").

In contrast to both stimulus and response definitions, a *stimulus-response* definition implies that "stress" refers to the overall process by which job demands impact employees. This process is depicted in Figure 1.1. When this definition is used, the term *stressor* is used to indicate job or organizational conditions that may require adaptive responses from employees, and *strain* is used to refer to a multitude of *negative* ways employees *may* respond when faced with stressors. If

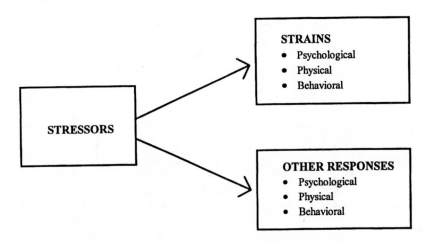

Figure 1.1. The Basic Process by Which Stressors May Lead to Strains and Other Responses

an employee's response to a stressor were either neutral or even positive (Payne, Jabri, & Pearson, 1988), such a response would not be considered a strain.

Strains are generally classified as psychological, physical, or behavioral. Examples of commonly studied psychological strains include such things as job dissatisfaction, anxiety, and depressed mood. Physical strains cover a broad spectrum ranging from minor somatic complaints (e.g., headaches, upset stomach) to more serious conditions such as coronary heart disease. Finally, behavioral strains include such things as absenteeism, poor performance, and turnover.

Occupational Stress Models

Over the years, many occupational stress researchers have put forth "models" of the process by which stress in the work environment impact employees. Models are useful primarily because they allow researchers to put their findings into some meaningful context. If not for theoretical models, most of our research would be of the "shotgun" variety, resulting in little scientific progress. One must keep in mind, however, that any attempt to model human behavior in any form is incomplete. Thus, it is best to think of all models as "approximations" of the processes they are trying to describe.

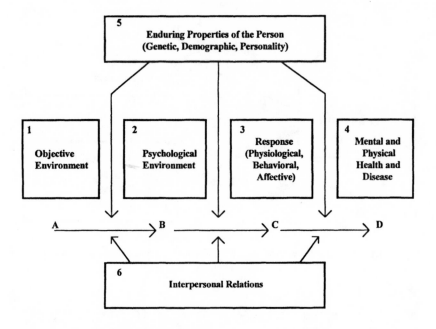

Figure 1.2. ISR Model of Work Stress
SOURCE: From Katz, D., & Kahn, R. L. (1978). *The social psychology of organizations* (2nd ed.). New York: John Wiley. Reprinted by permission of John Wiley & Sons, Inc.

One of the first occupational stress models came out of the previously mentioned program of research at the Institute for Social Research (ISR) at the University of Michigan (French & Kahn, 1962; Katz & Kahn, 1978). As can be seen in Figure 1.2, the ISR model, as it is usually referred to, begins with the *objective environment.* This simply includes anything in the organizational environment that may be perceived by employees; for example, the arrangement of the desks in an office is a part of the objective environment. The next step in the model, *psychological environment,* represents the process by which individuals perceive the objective environment. That is, employees make some *appraisal* of the objective environment.

Once the environment is appraised, there may be immediate physiological, behavioral, and affective (emotional) responses on the part of the employee. Physiological responses may include increased heart rate and blood pressure. Behavioral responses may include decreased effort and withdrawal from the workplace. Affective responses may include reduced levels of job satisfaction and increases in depressive symptoms. Depending on the nature of the physiological, behavioral, or affective responses to the environment, there may be adverse changes in mental and physical health, as well as disease. Such changes would be considered "strains," according to this model. For example, physiological changes such as increased heart rate and elevated blood pressure may ultimately lead to coronary heart disease (CHD).

The other two components of the model (5 and 6) illustrate the fact that the processes depicted in the rest of the model may be different for different individuals. For example, people may differ in terms of genetic makeup, demographic characteristics, and personality traits. People also differ in terms of the quality of their interpersonal relations with others in an organization. Such differences may affect perceptions of the work environment, as well as reactions to those perceptions.

Although the ISR model has proven to be quite useful to occupational stress researchers over the years, there are other models that more directly examine the performance implications of job-related stressors. Chief among these is McGrath's (1976) process model. As shown in Figure 1.3, McGrath conceptualized organizational stress as a four-stage, closed-loop process. The first stage, like the ISR model, represents situations that employees encounter in organizations. These situations are then perceived via the appraisal process. As with the ISR model, when these perceptions are negative, the existence of a stressor(s) is indicated. Once a situation is appraised, individuals make decisions as to how they will respond. Once a response is chosen, individuals then engage in some form of behavior and, by doing so, may alter the original situation. When such behavioral responses are negative (e.g., reduced effort), they are considered to be strains.

The relevance of McGrath's (1976) model to the issue of occupational stress and job performance is quite obvious. Specifically, this model tells us that when employees perceive a stressor in the work environment, they may decide to engage in behaviors that detract from their job performance. For example, an employee confronted with an unsafe work environment may perceive this to be a stressor. The employee may therefore decide not to put forth as much effort on the job. If this employee ultimately does withhold effort, this will likely reduce his or her job performance.

An extension of McGrath's (1976) theoretical model that is helpful in understanding the performance implications of occupational stress was proposed by Beehr and Bhagat (1985). According to these researchers, many stressors in organizations are due to employee uncertainty with respect to: (a) whether their effort will lead to high levels of job performance ($E \rightarrow P$) and (b) whether high

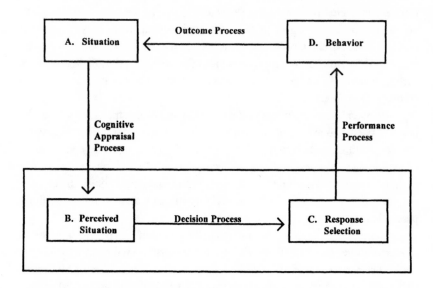

Figure 1.3. McGrath's Process Model of Work Stress
SOURCE: From McGrath, J. E. (1976). Stress and behavior in organizations. In M. D. Dunnette (Ed.), *Handbook of industrial and organizational psychology* (pp. 1351-1395). Chicago: Rand McNally. Reprinted by permission of Marvin D. Dunnette.

levels of job performance will lead to valued outcomes (P → O). Furthermore, such uncertainty must last for a relatively long duration in order to be harmful to employees (i.e., lead to strains).

What happens if an employee is uncertain for a long period of time about whether high levels of effort will lead to correspondingly high levels of job performance? It seems quite likely that, in such a situation, a logical response for an employee would be to withhold effort. What about extended periods of uncertainty regarding performance-outcome relations? Again, to the extent that an employee is rational (which, of course, may not always be the case), there would not appear to be a compelling reason for such an individual to perform exceptionally well. It is quite easy to see that Beehr and Bhagat's (1985) theory is useful in explaining why stressors may be followed by performance decrements.

A model of occupational stress that has received considerable attention, especially in research on the relationship between occupational stress and cardiovascular disease, is Karasek's (1979) demand-control model. Simply stated, this theory posits that the most stressful situations in the workplace are those in which employees have many demands but, at the same time, have low levels of control over their work (Karasek used the term "Job Decision Latitude"). A good example of this might be an employee on a factory assembly line. Such an individual may have very demanding production quotas to meet but, at the same time, have very little control over such things as the work pace of others and the reliability of machinery.

While most research on the demand-control model has examined health and physiological outcomes (e.g., Karasek, Baker, Marxer, Ahlbom, & Theorell, 1981; Perrewe & Ganster, 1989), it is also quite possible that job performance would suffer in situations where demands are high and control is low. Going back to the example of the factory worker, level of performance should largely be a function of things in the environment that the employee cannot control (e.g., work pace of others, reliability of machinery). Thus, if others work at a reasonable pace and there are no problems with machinery, employee performance should not be impaired. It is likely, however, that such high demand-low control situations may engender feelings of tension, depression, alienation, and even apathy (Salvendy, 1972). Such feelings may, in turn, ultimately detract from job performance.

A final model of occupational stress, which actually has implications for many organizational phenomena, is that of person-environment (P-E) fit. The historical roots of the P-E fit model date back to the well-known social psychologist Kurt Lewin and his notion of *interactional psychology*. Lewin's notion was simply that behavior is a function of the interaction between the person and the situation (e.g., B = f[P, S]). Of course, one aspect of this interaction between persons and situations is the degree to which the person *fits* with the situation. According to Kristof (1996), there are several different dimensions along which fit can be measured. For instance, it can be measured between an employee's skills/abilities and job requirements. Logically, one would assume that a job would lead to strain if it required skills and abilities that the person did not possess. Conversely, a job requiring a skill/ability level that is considerably *lower* than that possessed by the employee could also lead to strains due to boredom and understimulation.

The notion of P-E fit can also be conceptualized at a more "macro" level. For example, each employee brings a somewhat different set of *values* to the work-place. Some employees may place a high value on family and a comparatively low value on career success. Conversely, others may view career success as relatively more important than family. At the same time, organizations have a set of values that guides many decisions and policies. In some cases, these values can be traced directly to the founder of the organization, while in other cases they evolve over time and may change in response to external pressures.

According to the P-E fit model, strain may result from large differences between employee and organizational values. This is not to say that employee and organizational values must be identical, but if an employee works for an organization with values *extremely* different from his or her own, it is quite possible this may cause the employee to experience a variety of strains over time. To illustrate this point, a person who places a very high value on individual accomplishment would probably find it difficult to work for an organization that places a very high value on team performance and accomplishment.

At this point, several models of occupational stress have been reviewed. These represent a comprehensive, though certainly not exhaustive, set of theoretical models that have guided much occupational stress research. What major implications may be drawn from these theoretical models? That is, what do they tell us about the way researchers approach the study of occupational stress?

One clear implication is that *perceptions mediate the impact of the objective work environment.* That is, most occupational stress models posit that in order for something in an organization to be a "stressor," it must be perceived and labeled as such by the employee. The importance of perceptual processes is certainly reflected in the popularity of self-report measures of job-related stressors. Another implication is that *people are active participants in the occupational stress process.* That is, employees make decisions about how to respond to stressors in the work environment (Beehr & Bhagat, 1985; McGrath, 1976), and such responses may alter the work environment (French & Kahn, 1962). A final implication from these models is that *individual differences have an impact on both the perception of stressors and the reactions to these stressors.* This is probably most explicit in the ISR model but is implicitly part of the other models as well.

Conclusion

This chapter was designed to provide the reader with a concise overview of the field of occupational stress. This was done by providing a brief history of this field, introducing important terms and concepts, and describing important models of the stress process. After completing this chapter, the reader should have a much better understanding of the scientific study of occupational stress. Such an understanding will help as we ultimately narrow the focus to the relationship between stressors and job performance in the following chapters.

2

Stressors in the Workplace

I t is likely that most readers of this book are either currently employed or have been at some point in their lives. Based on that employment experience, most would probably agree that there are many potential "stressors" in the workplace. The major objective of this chapter is to describe several important workplace stressors. In addition to a clear definition for each stressor will be an explanation of how it may be caused and a description of how it is typically measured. A sample item is provided for each of the measures described.

Deciding which stressors to include in this chapter was difficult. One factor that influenced this decision was that most of the stressors described in this chapter have been discussed in comprehensive reviews of the occupational stress literature (e.g., Beehr & Newman, 1978; Ivancevich & Matteson, 1980; Jex & Beehr, 1991; Kahn & Byosiere, 1992). Also, the stressors covered in this chapter correspond closely with those identified by the National Institute of Occupational Safety and Health as important *psychosocial risk factors* (or stressors) in the workplace

9

TABLE 2.1 The National Institute of Occupational Safety and Health Taxonomy of Psychosocial Risk Factors

1. Work load and work pace
2. Work schedule
3. Role stressors
4. Career security factors
5. Interpersonal factors
6. Job context

(Sauter, Murphy, & Hurrell, 1990; also see Table 2.1). The reader can thus be assured that the stressors covered in this chapter are those that have received the attention of occupational stress researchers.

Role Stressors

A *role* can be defined as a set of behaviors that are expected of a person occupying a particular position. Most of us play multiple roles in life (e.g., parent, employee, spouse, community member) and thus have multiple sets of behavioral expectations. In social systems such as organizations, roles serve the important function of coordinating individual members' behavior (Katz & Kahn, 1978). Without roles, most organizations would function very poorly or even cease to exist.

Employees in organizations receive role-related information through both formal and informal sources. The most typical formal sources of role-related information are written job descriptions and communication with immediate supervisors. The information gleaned from these information sources, however, does not completely define an employee's role. For example, many readers will note that their formal job description may differ considerably from what they actually do on their job. This is because there are many other sources of role-related information, including subordinates, coworkers at the same level, and even customers. The term *role set* is used to denote the various sources that communicate role-related information to employees.

Ideally, role-related information is clearly communicated to employees, and the members of a role set provide consistent information. Unfortunately, this does not always happen. When role-related information is unclear, this may lead to a stressor known as *role ambiguity* (King & King, 1990; Kahn et al., 1964). To appreciate fully the nature of role ambiguity, it is useful to think about starting a new job. Those who have recently gone through this experience would likely attest to the fact that this is a time of considerable uncertainty that, for most people, is stressful (Beehr & Bhagat, 1985). Fortunately, the stress associated with starting a new job is tempered by the fact that the performance expectations for brand-new employees are usually rather low. Unfortunately for many employees, role ambiguity is a consistent feature of their jobs.

Role ambiguity may occur for a number of reasons. First, organizations may simply be lax in revising outdated or poorly written job descriptions. Because these job descriptions are often the first source of role-related information for a new employee, this may start the new employee off with a sense of ambiguity and confusion. Second, some roles are simply more difficult to define than others. This is especially true of managerial positions (Campbell, Dunnette, Lawler, & Weick, 1970). In many organizations, managers are held accountable for certain results (e.g., achieving a certain level of profitability) but are given very little guidance as to the behaviors required to achieve those results.

A third common cause of role ambiguity is environmental change, because the content of many organizational roles is linked to factors and events outside of the organization. When these change, the requirements of the role often change or become unclear. For example, societal expectations of educational institutions have changed considerably in recent years. Educational institutions, at all levels, are now expected to shape students' values and attitudes, in addition to providing them with the basic skills needed to become productive members of society. Such changes in societal expectations may lead to considerable role ambiguity on the part of educators; that is, members of this profession may ask themselves questions such as: How far should I go in shaping students' values? What are the "correct" values to be taught? What is the correct balance between shaping values and teaching basic skills?

The assessment of role ambiguity (like the other stressors in this chapter) has been almost exclusively through self-report measures. By far the most widely used measure of role ambiguity has been the scale developed by Rizzo, House, and Lirtzman (1970). A sample item from this scale is, "I know what my responsibilities are." If an employee were to disagree strongly with this statement, this would be indicative of role ambiguity. Despite much debate over the years regarding the relative merits of this scale (e.g., Kelloway & Barling, 1990; Netemeyer, Johnston, & Burton, 1990; Smith, Tisak, & Schmieder, 1993; Tracy & Johnson, 1981), there have been few efforts to develop alternative measures.

An alternative role ambiguity scale that may prove quite useful to occupational stress researchers was recently developed by Breaugh and Colihan (1994). One of the nice features of this scale is that it breaks role ambiguity (they label it "Job Ambiguity") into three dimensions that are represented by three subscales (*Work Method Ambiguity:* "I know how to get my work done"; *Scheduling Ambiguity:* "I know when I should be doing a particular aspect [part] of my job"; and *Performance Criteria Ambiguity:* "I know what my supervisor considers satisfactory work performance"). As with the item from the Rizzo et al. (1970) scale, disagreement with these statements indicates higher levels of role ambiguity.

Measuring multiple facets of role ambiguity makes sense because this stressor can be manifested in a variety of ways (King & King, 1990). The Breaugh and Colihan scale therefore allows for more precise measurement of role ambiguity. This greater precision ultimately provides organizations with greater diagnostic information than the Rizzo et al. (1970) scale because it helps pinpoint specific ways in which ambiguity can be reduced (e.g., clarifying performance expectations). Furthermore, in limited use it has been shown to have acceptable measurement properties (Allen & Jex, 1995; Heinisch & Jex, 1996).

Another problem that may occur as employee roles develop is that role-related information provided by one member of a role set may conflict with the information provided by another member. When this happens, the stressor that results is *role conflict* (Kahn et al., 1964). In occupational stress research, the form of role conflict that is studied most often is *intra-role* conflict. This simply means that an individual receives conflicting messages pertaining to one role. For example, a salesperson may be told by one manager to spend more time prospecting for new customers, whereas another manager may feel more time should be spent providing service to existing customers. This form of role conflict can be distinguished from *inter-role* conflict, which refers to competing role demands that arise from different roles. A very pertinent example of this is the tension that often results from the competing demands of work and family (Frone, Russell, & Cooper, 1991). The topic of inter-role conflict will not be covered here, because there are other excellent sources of information about this stressor elsewhere (e.g., Cartwright & Cooper, 1997; Greenhaus & Parasuraman, 1986; Gupta & Jenkins, 1985).

What causes a person to experience role conflict? Most often this is due to poor communication and coordination among role senders (Schaubroeck, Ganster, Sime, & Ditman, 1993). In many organizations, information flow is poorly coordinated, and as a result, an employee may receive conflicting information from members of his or her role set. I can recall this occurring frequently to fellow graduate students during their dissertation research when the members of their dissertation committee would make different, and sometimes conflicting, suggestions.

In some cases, however, role conflict is unavoidable because of characteristics inherent in a particular role. Many people occupy what are termed *boundary-spanning* roles in organizations (Katz & Kahn, 1978). Such roles require that an employee frequently interact with and respond to individuals and groups both inside and outside of an organization. Unfortunately, the demands of these various groups and individuals may be conflicting. A good example of a boundary-spanning role is that of an elected official in a democratic government. An inherent feature of this role is that the occupant often must balance the competing demands of the electorate and of special interest groups (e.g., corporations, unions, trade associations).

As is the case with role ambiguity, the problem of role conflict may also be intensified by environmental changes. In response to change, organizational roles become more complex, which greatly increases the potential for role conflict. A good example of this is the changing role of coaches in professional sports. In the past, coaches functioned primarily as authority figures and exerted considerable control over players. More recently, due to changing views regarding authority and to escalating salaries, coaching at this level has become much more complex. As a result, coaches must often mediate between the often competing demands of maintaining authority and keeping players happy.

Like role ambiguity, the assessment of role conflict has been primarily through self-report measurement. The scale that has been used most often is that developed by Rizzo et al. (1970). These items ask respondents whether they experience things such as "incompatible requests" and situations in which their work is "accepted by one group but not accepted by others." A sample item from this scale is, "I receive incompatible requests from two or more people." Strong agreement with a statement such as this indicates a high level of role conflict. Like the Rizzo et al. role ambiguity scale, this scale has also been the focus of much criticism and debate in the occupational stress literature (Kelloway & Barling, 1990; Netemeyer et al., 1990; Smith et al., 1993; Tracy & Johnson, 1981). Unfortunately, there have been few attempts to develop alternative measures.

A third role stressor that has been examined in the occupational stress literature is *role overload*, which is defined by Jones, Flynn, and Kelloway (1995) as a stressor that occurs when "an employer may demand more of an employee than he or she can reasonably accomplish in a given time, or simply, the employee may perceive the demands of work as excessive" (p. 42). To understand role overload, it is useful to distinguish between *quantitative* and *qualitative* role overload. When quantitative role overload is experienced, the employee is fully capable of meeting role demands. The problem is simply that there are too many role demands for the employee to handle. Given more time, and perhaps resources, the employee who is quantitatively overloaded could meet his or her role demands. On the other hand, when an employee is qualitatively overloaded, the demands of the role exceed his or her skills and abilities. In this case, even with more time and resources, the employee would not be able to meet his or her role demands.

There are several factors that may contribute to both quantitative and qualitative role overload. Organizational downsizing, for example, may lead to understaffing (Jick, 1985). This, in turn, may increase the quantitative role demands of those who remain in the organization (Kozlowski, Chao, Smith, & Hedlund, 1993). Quantitative role overload may also occur because of understaffing due to more transient situational factors. For example, if one member of a particular work group is either dismissed or leaves the organization for another position, the other members within that group usually must pick up the slack until a replacement is hired and trained.

Even when staffing levels are adequate, employees may still be quantitatively overloaded due to poor job design or poor communication among role senders. Jobs may be designed in a variety of ways, depending on the outcome an organization is trying to maximize (e.g., efficiency, motivation, employee comfort, employee information processing; Campion & Thayer, 1985). If a job is designed to maximize employee motivation but it completely ignores efficiency, an employee may be highly motivated yet overloaded. Poor communication among role senders can also result in quantitative role overload in cases in which role demands may be compatible but, taken together, are excessive.

In the case of qualitative role overload, individuals' skills and abilities do not allow them to meet their role demand adequately. This may occur for two reasons. As described in Chapter 1, the P-E fit model of occupational stress concerns the match between employees and the job environment. One form of P-E fit (or in this case, *misfit*) is that between an individual's *abilities* and the demands of a job (Kristof, 1996). An example of this would be an engineering student with a low level of spatial ability. In this case, much of the coursework would likely exceed this student's capabilities. Poor P-E fit of this type is often due to errors in the employee selection process, because of the importance of ability as a predictor of performance in many jobs (e.g., Schmidt & Hunter, 1978). It is also unlikely that abilities can be modified through training or experience.

There may also be a lack of fit between employees' *skills* and the demands of a job. Unlike abilities, skills are more amenable to modification through training and experience. Thus, P-E fit of this type is often due to problems with employee training. According to Goldstein (1993), many organizations do not train employees adequately. For example, training programs are either poorly designed or designed in a way that does not meet the needs of employees. Either way, employees may be inadequately prepared to meet their role demands.

Like the other two role stressors covered in this chapter, role overload is most often assessed through self-report questionnaires. One popular role overload measure is a scale developed by Caplan et al. (1975). As would be expected, these items appropriately reflect the frequency and intensity of role demands (e.g., "How much workload do you have?"). Respondents would typically respond to these items on a scale ranging from "very light" to "extremely heavy." Despite the popularity of this measure, there are undoubtedly other ways to measure role overload that employ non-self-report methods. These will be discussed in the next section, which focuses on the more general issue of employee workload.

Workload

Workload can be defined as simply the amount of work an employee has to do. This definition, however, is deceptively simple for three reasons. First, to truly understand workload, it is necessary to distinguish between *perceptions* of workload and *actual* workload. That is, two employees may have the same number of tasks to complete, but one may perceive his or her workload to be higher than the other. Second, for many jobs workload is cyclical. Tax accountants, for example, experience a sharp increase in workload as the deadline for filing tax returns approaches. As McGrath and Beehr (1990) aptly point out, this is true of many other variables in occupational stress research. Unfortunately, in most research, all variables are measured at one point in time so there is no way to assess these cyclical changes. Finally, as with role overload, it is necessary to distinguish between the sheer volume of work one is required to perform (quantitative workload) and the difficulty of the work (qualitative workload).

Given their close connection, workload is undoubtedly affected by many of the same factors that impact role overload. However, occupational stress researchers typically examine workload as a distinct stressor because it is affected by demands that require no "role-sending" processes. For example, the workload of a design engineer is likely to be affected by role-related demands from others. On the other hand, such an individual's workload may also be influenced by the inherent complexity of his or her job tasks. This is true of many jobs that require employees to use very high-level mental skills. This is not meant to imply that the relationship between job complexity and strain is necessarily linear (i.e., as complexity increases, stress increases). According to Xie and Johns (1995), for example, jobs are experienced as stressful when they are either *very low* or *very high* in complexity. In the case of low complexity, the stress may result from boredom, whereas high complexity may lead to mental fatigue and exhaustion. Either way, the result may be negative.

Workload may be measured either objectively or subjectively. Objective workload measures might include hours of work, number of projects, number of clients served, or, possibly, number of products produced. Objective workload measures are appealing because they do not require any interpretation on the part of employees. Unfortunately, most objective measures are rather crude indicators of workload. Hours of work probably provides the best illustration of this point. Some readers may be able to think of an example of a coworker who puts in many hours in the office but actually accomplishes very little. In this case, hours would be a poor indicator of that person's workload.

Subjective measures are based on employees' perceptions of their level of workload. A subjective workload scale developed by Spector, Dwyer, and Jex (1988) asks for respondents' perceptions of workload both in terms of quantity ("How often is there a great deal to be done?") and quality ("How often do you have to do work that you really don't know how to do?"). Responses to these items would typically be on a scale ranging from "very infrequently" to "very frequently." The advantage of this type of measure is that it acknowledges the fact that workload is somewhat subjective. Unfortunately, like any self-report measure, responses to such scales may be influenced by factors other than the work environment (Spector, 1992). Ultimately, the best way to measure workload is some combination of objective and subjective measures.

Interpersonal Conflict

Most jobs involve some interaction with other people (e.g., coworkers, contractors, customers), and such interactions can be a source of satisfaction and fulfillment (Spector, 1997a). Unfortunately, at times interactions with others can make work more stressful when they result in *interpersonal conflict* (Keenan & Newton, 1985). The intensity of interpersonal conflict can range from minor disagreements between coworkers to heated arguments. In the extreme, interpersonal conflicts may even lead to physical violence.

Several factors in the workplace may increase the probability of interpersonal conflict. For example, it has been well established in the social psychological literature (see Forsyth, 1990) that competition is often a precursor to conflict. Therefore, two employees may not get along well because they are competing for the same promotion. Competition may also be heightened when employees must compete for scarce organizational resources. In many organizations, the budget allocation process creates what is termed a *zero-sum game*. That is, the more Department A receives, the less Department B will be allocated. When this is the case, interpersonal conflict is often a by-product.

Interpersonal conflict may also be more likely to occur when an employee feels that he or she is being treated unfairly or unprofessionally by a coworker. This may be through expressions of rudeness or disrespect. In work groups, such feelings of unfairness may also be engendered by what is termed *free riding* among group members (Albanese & Van Fleet, 1985; Roberts, 1995). Free riding is simply the tendency on the part of some work group members not to "pull their weight," which requires the more hardworking group members to pick up the slack. Those picking up the slack may resent the free rider, and the result may be interpersonal conflict among group members.

In some work situations, interpersonal conflict may still be present even though conditions that foster competition may be minimal and coworkers treat each other with fairness and respect. In such cases, interpersonal conflict may largely be due to stable individual differences among coworkers. According to Swap and Rubin (1983), some people are naturally more competitive (labeled "Competitors") than others (labeled "Cooperators"). Thus, a group composed of a large number of naturally competitive people may have a high degree of interpersonal conflict, despite favorable situational influences. In cases like this, the best way to minimize interpersonal conflict would possibly be to change the composition of the group.

Like the other stressors in this chapter, interpersonal conflict is typically assessed with self-report measures. One such scale was developed by Spector (1987). A sample item from this scale is, "How often do you get into arguments with others at work?" Like the previously described workload scale, responses to these items might range from "very infrequently" to "very frequently." Although the items on this scale certainly reflect those things we normally associate with interpersonal conflict (e.g., getting into arguments, rudeness), the scale includes only *overt* forms of interpersonal conflict. This is a limitation because, in some cases, employees may engage in conflict in more covert ways, such as spreading rumors about each other or perhaps refusing to take the initiative to help each other.

Situational Constraints

The effectiveness of organizations depends largely on the job performance of individual employees (Campbell, 1990). Thus, it is in an organization's best interest to create organizational conditions that facilitate individuals' job performance. Unfortunately, organizations may inadvertently fail to do this at times. The result is that "situational constraints" are imposed on employees. Peters and O'Connor (1980) define situational constraints as any conditions in an employee's immediate work environment that inhibit or constrain performance. Situational constraints essentially prevent employees from translating skills, abilities, and motivation into high levels of job performance.

Peters and O'Connor (1988) identified 11 primary categories of situational constraints in organizations: (a) job-related information, (b) budgetary support, (c) required support, (d) materials and supplies, (e) required services and help from others, (f) task preparation, (g) time availability, (h) the work environment, (i) scheduling of activities, (j) transportation, and (k) job-relevant authority. For any of these categories of constraints, the inhibiting effect on performance may be due to unavailability, inadequacy, or poor quality.

To illustrate more clearly how situational constraints might inhibit performance, take the example of job-related information. A detective trying to solve a crime may be unable to do so simply because of lacking information. That is, the criminal may have left no clues, and there are no witnesses. However, it is also possible that clues and witnesses are available, but they are either inadequate or of poor quality. For example, the detective may receive a tip that the criminal has fled to "another state," or witnesses may "think" they spotted the criminal. In both cases, the information may be of some value but, by itself, would probably not lead to the apprehension of the suspect.

Based on my own experiences as an employee, researcher, and consultant, situational constraints seem to be very common in today's organizations. One reason for this, as was discussed in the section on role overload, is organizational downsizing. When organizations reduce staffing levels, layoff survivors may lose access to needed support personnel and, as a result, their performance may suffer. Also, the increasing role demands that often confront layoff survivors may result in less time available for task accomplishment.

Another frequent cause of situational constraints (in fact this is even considered a *type* of situational constraint) is organizational budget cutting (Jick, 1985; Jick & Murray, 1982). Businesses, for example, are facing an increasingly competitive global marketplace, and often the only way to survive is to cut costs

(Kozlowski et al., 1993). Public institutions such as governments and schools are simply receiving less funding. Ironically, this has come at a time when the public seems to be demanding more accountability and higher levels of service from these same institutions.

According to Jick and Murray (1982), the impact of budget cuts depends on two major factors: (a) the size of the cuts and (b) whether or not an organization has anticipated the cuts. Budget cutting will lead to the most situational constraints and other negative consequences when cuts are both *large* and *unanticipated*. Even when unanticipated, small budget cuts will likely not have much of an effect because most organizations have some "slack" built into their budgetary system (Moorhead & Griffin, 1995). Large cuts are more problematic; however, the impact can be reduced if an organization has time to prepare.

On the other hand, large cuts that are *unanticipated* lead to the most situational constraints because little time is available for creating contingency plans. As a result, budgetary resources would likely be appropriated for only those things that are deemed absolutely essential. Going back to the Peters and O'Connor (1988) classification of situational constraints, it is possible that many of these would not be worthy of budgetary resources during such times. For example, preventative maintenance of equipment may be ignored, which eventually leads to a shutdown in production. In addition, required services (e.g., use of temporary clerical support) may be reduced or eliminated completely, thus further inhibiting task performance.

Another cause of situational constraints that is somewhat related to budget cutting is inadequate employee training. It is important to point out, though, that this is separate from budget cutting. Although training is affected by budgetary concerns, it is also strongly affected by other factors. According to Goldstein (1993), some organizations simply place a higher value on training than others. In addition, some organizational environments strongly support the transfer of training to the actual job, while others do not (Tracey, Tannenbaum, & Kavanaugh, 1995).

Regardless of the reasons for inadequate training, it may indirectly lead to many forms of situational constraints. An employee who is poorly trained obviously also stands a good chance of performing his or her job poorly. This not only has implications for the poorly trained employee, but for other employees as well. This is especially true if the poorly trained employee is responsible for providing needed services to others.

A final cause of situational constraints worth mentioning is simply temporary unanticipated events that are often part of organizational life. Several years ago at the university at which I worked, all of the clerical employees went on strike because of a dispute over their collective bargaining agreement. As luck would have it, I was working on a major revision of a manuscript at the time, so this was a major situational constraint (although I developed a new appreciation for the clerical staff!). This is obviously an unusual situation, but things do happen on occasion that cannot be controlled (e.g., accidents, bad weather, computer shut-downs).

A frequently used measure of situational constraints is an 11-item scale developed by Spector et al. (1988). Essentially, what these researchers did was create the items based on the previously described categories of situational constraints (Peters & O'Connor, 1980, 1988). Spector and colleagues also added one constraint (interruptions from others) to their scale that was not part of Peters and O'Connor's taxonomy. A sample item from the Spector et al. scale is, "How often do you find it difficult or impossible to do your job because of poor equipment or supplies?" Responses to these items can range from "never" to "daily."

I have used this scale in past research (e.g., Jex, 1988; Jex & Gudanowski, 1992), and one concern I have is whether the items may be too "generic." In other words, the items on this scale may not address the most important situational constraints for an individual holding a particular job in a particular organization. To be sure, this is a general issue in the measurement of all stressors (cf. Beehr, Jex, Stacy, & Murray, 1997). Therefore, if some of the items seem to lack relevance in a given setting, it would probably be prudent to supplement them with "locally developed" situational constraints items. Also, given the nature of situational constraints, it is quite possible to supplement self-report measures with more objective indexes (e.g., number of machine failures, incidence of computer shut-downs).

Perceived Control

The notion that humans desire control over their environment is well supported in the behavioral science literature (e.g., Averill, 1973). In fact, it has even been shown that simply having the *illusion* of control is comforting (Friedland, Keinan, & Regev, 1992). Maintaining feelings of control is also important in the workplace, and employees tend to find it stressful when they lack a sense of control (Spector, 1986).

Compared with the stressors covered up to this point, perceived control is much more general and can be manifested in many ways. According to Spector (1986), the two most common ways that perceived control is manifested in organizations is through *job autonomy* and *participative decision making*. An employee with a high level of job autonomy typically has discretion over how his or her job tasks will be performed and perhaps even over things like starting and ending times (Hackman & Oldham, 1980). University professors, for example, have considerable autonomy as to how they carry out their job tasks, whereas manual laborers typically do not. In light of this example, it is worth noting that job level and autonomy are related (Spector, Jex, & Chen, 1995), although not perfectly. For example, as a college student, I held a job as a night security guard for a newspaper company. This job provided considerable autonomy, even though it required very little of the incumbent other than dependability.

When considering job autonomy, it is also important to realize that the same job may have more or less job autonomy depending on the organization or even the department. Thus, variation in job autonomy depends not only on the general characteristics of a given job type but also on the way in which that job is designed in a particular setting. As an example, in the past many of the quarterbacks in the National Football League were responsible for selecting their team's offensive plays. Today, however, responsibility for play calling rests with the coaching staffs.

Participative decision making is defined by Lowin (1968) as an organizational form of decision making in which those who are responsible for carrying out decisions have some input into their formulation. This could be through mechanisms such as labor-management committees, quality circles, job enrichment, and other shared governance policies (Cotton, 1995). Some, however, have argued that true participative decision making consists primarily of supervisors consulting informally with subordinates before making major decisions (see Wagner, 1994). Regardless of the form, the logic behind participation is that those who are responsible for implementing decisions often have valuable insight to contribute.

In considering perceived control, whether in the form of job autonomy or participation, it is essential to consider the impact of individual differences. That is, to some employees a lack of perceived control is stressful, whereas to others it is not. This is an issue with all stressors (see Chapter 5), and it is mentioned here because there is evidence that considerable variation exists as to whether people desire control in the workplace (Alluto & Belasco, 1972; Fisher, 1995; Hackman & Oldham, 1980; Ivancevich, 1979). Given this impact of individual differences, it is probably best to think of perceived control in terms of the P-E fit model of stress discussed in Chapter 1. In this framework, stress is caused when an employee has either *too little* or *too much* control in the workplace.

The measurement of perceived control flows directly from the two primary manifestations of this stressor, which were discussed previously. The most popular measure of job autonomy has been the three-item autonomy scale taken from Hackman and Oldham's (1975) Job Diagnostic Survey, which was subsequently revised by Idaszak and Drasgow (1987). The items on this scale basically assess the amount of discretion an employee has in carrying out his or her job tasks (e.g., "The job gives me considerable opportunity for independence and freedom in how I do the work"). To the extent that a respondent disagrees with this item, autonomy (and hence perceived control) is lacking. One of the nice features of this scale is that it has been so widely used that Hackman and Oldham (1980) have published comparative data that allow users of the scale to compare scores they obtain to scores obtained from others in similar jobs.

Participative decision making has been measured using a variety of scales. A commonly used participation scale developed by Steel and Mento (1987) focuses on supervisor-subordinate interactions within work groups. A sample item is, "My supervisor usually asks for my opinions and thoughts on decisions affecting my work." A respondent who strongly disagreed with this statement would perceive a lack of control over his or her work. In most cases, such a scale will suffice. Unfortunately, in some cases this scale may lack relevance if a respondent does not have a formal "supervisor" or perhaps does not work in a group. Also, the items do not assess more formal manifestations of participation such as labor-management committees or perhaps quality circles.

A third approach to the measurement of perceived control is to assess it more directly. That is, rather than asking about job autonomy or participation, some scales ask respondents whether they feel a more general sense of control in the workplace. A scale of this type developed by Ashford, Lee, and Bobko (1989) does not address either job autonomy or participation in decisions. The items on this scale ask respondents whether, in a general sense, they feel they have control over events in the workplace. A sample item is, "I have enough power in this organization to control events that might affect my job." Strong disagreement with this item would indicate a lack of perceived control.

Despite the popularity of self-report measures of perceived control, there have been attempts to measure this stressor using other methods. For example, Ivancevich (1979) used a non-self-report measure of control based on the number of decisions employees were allowed to make, and Adelmann (1987) used job analysis ratings derived from the *Dictionary of Occupational Titles (DOT)* to examine the relationship between control and a number of strains. More recently, Spector and Jex (1991) assessed job autonomy through independent ratings of job descriptions.

Such non-self-report measures are useful because they are not affected by the biases of individual respondents (Spector, 1992). Ironically, the advantage of these measurement approaches leads to their major disadvantage. That is, when non-self-report measures are used, researchers are no longer assessing "perceived" control on the job. Ultimately, the best approach to measuring control in the workplace is to use both multiple methods and data sources (Jick, 1979).

Traumatic Job Stressors

Up to this point, all of the stressors that have been examined can be described as "chronic" stressors; that is, they are more or less a constant part of a person's job or job situation (Beehr & Newman, 1978). This initial focus on chronic stressors was because most occupational stress research over the years has been on examining the effects of such chronic stressors. Furthermore, chronic stressors do generalize to most jobs and organizational settings.

For certain types of jobs, however, chronic stressors may not be the most salient source of stress. Firefighters, law enforcement personnel, emergency medical personnel, physicians, and even teachers are routinely faced with stressors that differ markedly from those that have been covered. Examples of these might include exposure to death and suffering and perhaps even being required to harm another person (Allen & Jex, 1995). Other non-job-specific traumatic stressors examined in occupational stress literature include a plant explosion (Barling, 1987) and workplace violence (Elliott & Jarrett, 1994; Johnson & Indvik, 1994). All of these stressors are considered "traumatic" because they are clearly outside the range of normal experience and are likely to be distressing to almost anyone (Hillenberg & Wolf, 1988).

The lack of occupational stress research on traumatic stressors is unfortunate for a number of reasons (Allen & Jex, 1995). First, given the intensity of traumatic stressors, employee responses to them may be different than responses to more chronic stressors. Second, as mentioned above, traumatic stressors are common-place in some occupations. Thus, focusing exclusively on chronic stressors provides an incomplete understanding of stress among members of those occupations. Finally, there are few data on the interaction between chronic and traumatic stressors. This is an important "blind spot" in the occupational stress literature because even in occupations in which the potential for traumatic stressors is high, chronic stressors may also be present. It would be interesting, for example, to investigate whether chronic stressors intensify or attenuate the effects of traumatic stressors.

Conclusion

This chapter has covered the most commonly studied stressors in occupational stress research: role stressors, workload, interpersonal conflict, situational constraints, and perceived control. At this point, the reader should have a better understanding of (a) what these stressors are, (b) how they are caused, and (c) how they are measured. "Traumatic" stressors were also briefly covered, and the point was made that some stressors are highly occupation specific and may occur in a limited time frame.

Even though the stressors covered in this chapter are those that have commonly been studied, their inclusion is not meant to imply that they are the *only* stressors that occur in organizations. As was pointed out at the beginning of the chapter, there are probably an infinite number of potential stressors in the workplace. Those discussed in this chapter are simply those that have received some attention from occupational stress researchers.

Job Performance as an Outcome Variable

In the preceding two chapters, considerable attention was devoted to the process by which stressors impact employees and to describing the nature of those stressors. In this chapter the focus shifts to job performance, because an understanding of performance is crucial if we are to understand how it is influenced by job stressors. To this end, I will define what is meant by job performance, delineate the factors that impact performance, explore possible mechanisms by which stressors affect performance, and finally describe some complicating factors that need to be considered when assessing the relation between stressors and performance.

Defining and Modeling Job Performance

Job performance is a deceptively simple term. At the most general level, it could be defined simply as "all of the behaviors we engage in while at work." This is a poor definition, however, because people often engage in behaviors that are not specific job tasks while at work. For example, in a study of enlisted military personnel, Bialek, Zapf, and McGuire (1977) found that less than *half* of their work time was spent performing tasks that were specified in their job descriptions. Though some nontask behaviors may facilitate task accomplishment (e.g., developing relationships with coworkers), others obviously do not (e.g., making personal phone calls). Thus, if performance is defined simply in terms of behaviors performed while at work, many behaviors that have no relation to job performance would be included. On the other hand, defining job performance solely in terms of *task performance* would exclude much workplace behavior that may ultimately contribute to job performance.

A more precise way of defining job performance is in relation to organizational goals. According to Campbell (1990), job performance can be defined in terms of behaviors employees engage in at work. However, he goes a step further by stating that such behaviors must contribute to organizational goals in order to be considered in the domain of job performance. This is obviously more precise than simply defining performance as all behaviors that employees perform at work. On the other hand, it is less restrictive than defining job performance solely in terms of task performance. This is important because many behaviors that are not strictly considered part of task performance (i.e., those not in a person's formal job description) often contribute to organizational goals (Organ, 1994; Organ & Ryan, 1995).

It is also important to distinguish job performance from several related terms. According to Campbell (1990), job performance can (and should) be distinguished from *effectiveness, productivity,* and *utility.* Let us examine each of these in order. Effectiveness is defined as the *evaluation* of the *results* of an employee's job performance. This is an important distinction to make because effectiveness is determined by more than just employee job performance. For example, it is possible for an employee to perform very well but receive a poor performance rating (a measure of effectiveness) because he or she does not get along well with the person providing the rating.

Productivity is closely related to effectiveness. The difference is that productivity takes into account the *cost* of achieving a given level of effectiveness. For example, two organizations may achieve the same level of financial profit in a given year and thus would be equally *effective.* However, the organization that achieves this level of profit at the lower cost would be considered the most *productive.* This can also be seen at the individual level, when two employees have the same level of output, but one achieves this more efficiently than the other.

Finally, utility represents the *value* of a given level of performance, effectiveness, or productivity. On the surface, this definition may seem the same as that provided for effectiveness. Utility is somewhat different, though, because it is possible for an employee to achieve a high level of effectiveness (i.e., the results of performance are judged to be positive) and for utility to be low. That is, an organization simply may not place a high *value* on the level of effectiveness achieved by the employee.

At this point, one may get the impression that distinguishing among performance, effectiveness, productivity, and utility is simply a trivial exercise designed to keep academics employed. On the contrary, these are extremely important distinctions to make when one is interested in understanding the relationship between job-related stressors and performance. As will be shown in the next chapter, many studies that purport to examine the relation between stressors and "performance" are actually measuring "effectiveness." This is also important because employees typically have more control over performance than they have over effectiveness or utility. We will return to this point later in the chapter.

While it is certainly useful to define what is meant by the term *job performance,* it is even more useful to specify the actual behavioral dimensions that constitute job performance. In order to do this, *models* of job performance are needed. As you may remember from Chapter 1, a model is simply an abstraction of some thing or process. In the behavioral sciences, no model is complete or exhaustive. However, models are helpful in guiding theory development, and they allow researchers to make more informed predictions.

Efforts to model job performance have essentially been aimed at identifying a set of behavioral dimensions that are common to all jobs. Given the vast number of jobs that exist in the world, one might wonder why anyone would undertake such a task. The truth of the matter is, few have. However, modeling job performance is vitally important because so much research and practice in the organizational sciences center around *performance prediction.* The most obvious example of this is using tests and interviews to predict the future performance of job applicants. In other cases, researchers are interested in exploring whether attitudes, goals, or perhaps values predict performance. Most important, researchers who examine the relationship between stressors and job performance are essentially confronted with a performance prediction problem. In the following paragraphs, three recent models of job performance are described.

Campbell (1990, 1994) proposed a model whereby performance on all jobs can be broken down into the eight dimensions presented in Table 3.1. As can be seen, the first dimension is labeled *job-specific task proficiency.* This represents

TABLE 3.1 Campbell's (1990, 1994) Taxonomy of Higher-Order Performance
Dimensions

1. Job-specific task proficiency
2. Non-job-specific task proficiency
3. Written and oral communication task proficiency
4. Demonstrating effort
5. Maintaining personal discipline
6. Facilitating peer and team performance
7. Supervision/leadership
8. Management/administration

---

the degree to which an individual can perform the core tasks associated with his
or her job. As an example, behaviors such as counting money, making deposits,
and cashing checks would represent this type of behavior for a bank teller.

The second dimension in this model is labeled *non–job-specific task proficiency*. This represents behaviors that need to be performed by some or all members
of an organization but are not specific to one's particular job. College professors,
for example, are required to perform such ancillary tasks as advising students and
serving on university committees, in addition to their main tasks of instruction and
research.

The third dimension is labeled *written and oral communication task proficiency*. This dimension provides recognition of the fact that incumbents in most
jobs must communicate either in writing or verbally. For example, a physician and
a lawyer obviously perform very different job-specific tasks. Both, however, are
required to communicate orally with their patients and clients, respectively.

The fourth and fifth dimensions are labeled *demonstrating effort* and *maintaining personal discipline,* respectively. Demonstrating effort represents an employee's level of motivation and commitment to his or her job tasks. Whether
performing the job of street sweeper, firefighter, or physical therapist, there are
differences in the extent to which people exhibit commitment to their job tasks and
are willing to persist in order to accomplish difficult or unpleasant tasks. Maintaining personal discipline is simply the degree to which employees refrain from
negative behaviors such as rule infractions or substance abuse. These two dimensions, taken together, basically represent the degree to which an employee is a
"good citizen" in the workplace.

The sixth dimension is labeled *facilitating peer and team performance.* One aspect of this dimension is the degree to which an employee is helpful to his or her coworkers when they need assistance. It also represents the degree to which an employee is a "team player," that is, works to further the goals of his or her work group. As Campbell (1990) points out, this dimension would obviously have little relevance if one worked in complete isolation. For most jobs, however, this is more the exception than the rule.

The seventh and eighth dimensions are labeled *supervision/leadership* and *management/administration,* respectively. Both of these dimensions represent aspects of job performance that would apply only to jobs that have some supervisory responsibilities. Whether one is a supervisor in a bank, department store, or factory, there are certain common behaviors required. For example, most supervisors must help employees set goals, teach more effective work methods, or perhaps model appropriate behaviors. Most supervisory positions also require a multitude of administrative tasks such as controlling expenditures, obtaining additional resources, and representing one's unit within an organization.

In considering each of these dimensions of job performance, it is clear that all dimensions will not be relevant for all jobs. In fact, Campbell (1990) argues that only three (core task proficiency, demonstrating effort, and maintenance of personal discipline) are major performance components of *every* job. This model is still quite useful because it is more precise than simply defining performance as a "set of behaviors that support organizational goals."

A second model of job performance has been proposed by Murphy (1990). Although this model was specifically developed to facilitate an understanding of job performance in the military, it still has considerable relevance for many civilian jobs as well. As can be seen in Table 3.2, Murphy's model breaks performance down into four dimensions instead of eight. The first of these is labeled *task-oriented behaviors,* which closely mirrors the job-specific task proficiency dimension from Campbell's (1990) model. It is also reasonable to assume, for supervisory jobs, that this would include the dimensions related to supervision/leadership and management/administration. In essence, this represents performing the major tasks associated with one's job.

The second dimension is labeled *interpersonally oriented behaviors,* which represents all interpersonal transactions that occur on the job. Presumably, many interpersonal transactions in the workplace are task related. To the extent that this is the case, this dimension mirrors that of facilitating peer and team performance

TABLE 3.2 Murphy's (1990) Dimensions of the Performance Domain

1. Task-oriented behaviors
2. Interpersonally oriented behaviors
3. Down-time behaviors
4. Destructive/hazardous behaviors

in Campbell's (1990) model. On the other hand, many interpersonal transactions in the workplace are not directly task related. To the extent that this is true, this dimension also reflects the extent to which an employee generally maintains positive interpersonal relations with coworkers, an aspect of job behavior that is not explicitly part of Campbell's (1990) model.

The third dimension is labeled *down-time behaviors* and represents behaviors that lead the job incumbent to be absent from the work site. This would include things such as drug and alcohol abuse. A closely related set of behaviors is included in the fourth category, labeled *destructive/hazardous behaviors*. These would include such things as safety violations, accidents, and even sabotage. These dimensions are most closely related to the dimension of maintaining personal discipline in Campbell's (1990) model. In some cases, though, counterproductive behaviors may be due to a lack of effort (e.g., not taking the time to put on safety equipment), so this may also be related to the demonstrating effort dimension in Campbell's model. In considering the impact of negative behaviors on overall job performance, Murphy (1990) points out that engaging in these certainly has a negative effect. On the other hand, *refraining* from negative behaviors does not necessarily make one more effective.

Compared to Campbell's (1990, 1994) eight-dimension model, Murphy's (1990) four-dimension model is somewhat less useful for two reasons. First, Murphy's model was created very specifically to explain job performance among U.S. Navy personnel. Campbell's objective was to describe performance in a broader spectrum of jobs, although his model could certainly be used to describe job performance among military personnel. Second, the performance dimensions described by Murphy are considerably broader than those described by Campbell. The breadth of these dimensions increases the difficulty of making predictions about how various job-related stressors may have an impact.

A third way of modeling job performance comes from Organ's (1977, 1994) work on *organizational citizenship behavior*. Generally speaking, organizational citizenship behaviors represent those behaviors that are not part of one's formal job description (e.g., helping a co-worker who has been absent; being courteous to others). It is also the case that *refraining* from certain forms of behavior is considered to be within the realm of organizational citizenship (e.g., not complaining about trivial matters). Although such behaviors are not required, they are needed in order for work groups and organizations to be effective (George & Bettenhausen, 1990).

At this point, it is important to point out that the purpose of organizational citizenship behavior research was *not* to develop a model of job performance (see Organ, 1994, for an interesting discussion of the development of his research program). However, a discussion of organizational citizenship behavior is included in this chapter for two reasons. First, the many forms of citizenship behavior fit very well into both of the models of job performance previously discussed. For example, in Campbell's (1990) model, organizational citizenship behaviors could legitimately fit into *at least* three dimensions of job performance—demonstrating effort, maintaining personal discipline, and facilitating peer and team performance. In Murphy's (1990) model, organizational citizenship behaviors could basically fit into any dimension except task-oriented behaviors.

A second and more compelling reason for discussing organizational citizenship behavior is that stressors may impact important antecedents of such behaviors. For example, it has been found that job satisfaction is the strongest and most consistent correlate of many forms of organizational citizenship behavior (Organ & Ryan, 1995). It is also known, of course, that one of the most consistent effects of job stressors is their tendency to *reduce* employee job satisfaction (Jackson & Schuler, 1985; Jex & Beehr, 1991; Spector, 1997a). Therefore, a reduction in organizational citizenship behavior may be a logical performance-related response to stressors because of the reduction in job satisfaction that often accompanies stressors.

Another reason why stressors may impact organizational citizenship behaviors is that employees typically have more control over these compared to behaviors associated with "in-role" performance. As a result, there should be more variation in organizational citizenship behaviors compared to in-role behaviors (Johns, 1991). Thus, when an employee is confronted with a stressor, it would seem more logical that he or she would withhold organizational citizenship

behaviors rather than allow in-role performance to decline. Other problems with
in-role performance as an outcome variable will be discussed later in this chapter.

The Determinants of Job Performance

Now that we have a better understanding of what exactly is meant by job
performance, the next step is to develop an understanding of its antecedents. This
is important because, in many cases, stressors may not impact performance directly
(one exception would be situational constraints). Rather, stressors often have an
indirect impact on performance by influencing those factors that lead to differences
in job performance.

In trying to explain behavior, behavioral scientists have at times engaged in
heated debates over the relative impact of the person versus the environment (e.g.,
nature vs. nurture). In most cases, these debates are resolved by the rather
commonsense notion that most behavior is the result of a complex interaction
between characteristics of the person and characteristics of the environment. Thus,
it is from this starting point that the causes of job performance are examined.

Generally speaking, differences in performance are caused by the interaction
between ability, motivation, and situational factors that may facilitate or inhibit
performance (Muchinsky, 1993). Thus, for an employee to perform well, it is
certainly important for that person to possess job-relevant abilities. Ability alone
will not lead to high levels of performance, though, unless the employee is
motivated to perform and does not experience severe situational constraints. Of
course, in some cases, a high level of one of these three factors will compensate
for low levels of the others (e.g., a highly motivated employee will overcome
situational constraints), but usually all three conditions are necessary for performance to be at a consistently high level.

Drawing on this general notion, Campbell (1990) proposed that performance
is determined by the interaction between *declarative knowledge, procedural
knowledge/skill,* and *motivation.* Declarative knowledge is simply knowledge
about facts and things. An employee with a high level of declarative knowledge
has a good understanding of the tasks required by his or her job. Once an employee
has achieved a high degree of declarative knowledge, he or she is in a position to
acquire a high level of procedural knowledge/skill. When this is achieved, the
employee understands not only what needs to be done but also *how* to do it.
Differences in the acquisition of both declarative knowledge and procedural

knowledge/skills are strongly influenced by differences in employees' innate abilities.

When an employee has achieved a high degree of procedural knowledge/skill, he or she is *capable* of high levels of job performance. Of course, whether or not this capability is translated into high levels of job performance depends on motivation. This, according to Campbell (1990), reflects an employee's choices regarding (a) whether to expend effort directed at job performance, (b) the level of effort to expend, and (c) whether to persist with the level of effort chosen. Thus, even if an employee has achieved a very high level of procedural knowledge/skill, it may never be translated into a high level of performance due to low motivation. The primary value of Campbell's model is that it states, in precise terms, the factors within the person that determine performance. Unfortunately, the model essentially ignores situational factors.

Sternberg (1994) proposed a much more extensive model in which performance is determined by five general factors, labeled *Person, Roles, Situations, Values,* and *Luck.* As in Campbell's (1990) model, Sternberg's Person factor includes declarative knowledge, procedural knowledge/skill, and motivation. This factor included additional factors such as mental and physical abilities, preferred thinking and learning styles, and personality differences.

The Roles portion of this model is simply a recognition of the fact that performance is affected by an employee's level of comfort with the job-related role he or she is asked to play. According to Sternberg (1994), some people prefer to be leaders while others would rather be followers, some prefer to be managers while others prefer to be entrepreneurs, and so on. The major point is that performance is much more likely to be at a high level when one plays a preferred role.

The Situations portion of this model has to do with things in the job situation that may inhibit or facilitate performance. In describing situational influences, however, Sternberg's (1994) real focus is on the degree to which job situations *match* the abilities and preferences of employees. Thus, it is somewhat different than the concept of situational constraints (Peters & O'Connor, 1980) described in Chapter 2. An example of how situational influences might work in Sternberg's model is that a person may have a high level of ability for a particular job but not perform well because there is something about the job situation that he or she finds hard to tolerate. For example, a person may have considerable ability for clerical work but perform poorly in a department where there is considerable pressure to meet deadlines if that person does not prefer such an environment.

The Values portion of the model proposes that performance often depends on the degree to which the values of the person *match* the values of the organization. It has been shown that such a match is important in determining things such as commitment (O'Reilly, Chatman, & Caldwell, 1991); however, relatively little work has been done relating this to performance. Presumably, the match between organizational and employee values could impact performance in two ways. First, a mismatch in values may reduce motivation, which subsequently reduces performance. Second, a mismatch in values may lead an employee to direct his or her efforts in the wrong direction. For example, an employee who places a high value on the *quality* of his or her work may not perform well in an organization that places a high value on quantity of production and pays little attention to quality.

The final category, Luck, refers to a multitude of relatively uncontrollable factors that may impact performance. The inclusion of Luck in a scientific model may seem a bit odd to some readers. In my opinion, however, Sternberg (1994) is correct to include it because in many cases luck does impact performance. For example, most of us have probably had the experience of being in "the right place at the right time" or "the wrong place at the wrong time." Despite the explanatory value of Luck, it has relatively little if any predictive value. That is, any event that occurs randomly (we would assume that Luck would fit this definition) cannot be used to forecast or predict another event.

How Stressors Impact Performance

At this point, we have an understanding of job performance and the factors that affect it. The time has now come to explain the mechanisms by which job stressors may impact job performance. This is not an easy task, because most occupational stress researchers have made very general predictions about relations between stressors and job performance. As a result, relations between stressors and performance have been rather weak and inconsistent (this empirical literature will be summarized in Chapter 4). The following quote summarizes this issue quite succinctly: "The literature on stress and performance would benefit greatly if researchers concentrated on developing and evaluating theoretically derived link-ages between specific job stressors and the specific duties and responsibilities of employees in a particular organizational position" (Fried & Tiegs, 1995, p. 282). Of course, it is beyond the scope of this book to make predictions about relations between specific stressors and specific performance dimensions or antecedents of performance. Nevertheless, in this section three propositions will be put forth that

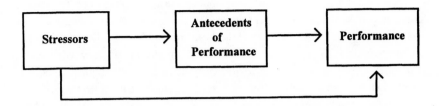

Figure 3.1. A Basic Model of the Process by Which Job Stressors Impact Job Performance

can be used when linking the job stressors discussed in Chapter 2 to job performance.

First, it is proposed that the mechanism by which most stressors impact job performance can be described as both *direct* and *indirect*. This general proposition is summarized in Figure 3.1. Some stressors, such as situational constraints, have a very direct inhibiting effect on performance (Peters & O'Connor, 1988). Many stressors, however, also affect performance indirectly by first impacting many of the previously described antecedents of performance (e.g., Campbell, 1990; Sternberg, 1994). Even in the case of situational constraints, the employee faced with such conditions may become frustrated and such frustration may serve to inhibit performance. In the case of role stressors, Beehr and Bhagat (1985) proposed that these may lead to uncertainty regarding employee perceptions of whether effort will lead to performance or whether performance will lead to meaningful outcomes. Such uncertainty, in turn, may impair performance because employees may be less likely to put forth effort under these conditions.

A second proposition, based on what is known about job performance, is that the effects of stressors are probably more *indirect* than *direct*. Going back to Figure 3.1, it is most often the case that stressors negatively impact job performance by first negatively impacting important antecedents. With the exception of situational constraints, most stressors do not result in immediate roadblocks to performance. This is because in many organizational settings there are several factors in place that serve to cut down on the variability of performance to begin with (Peters & O'Connor, 1988). Comparatively speaking, there is likely to be much more variability in the *antecedents* of performance (e.g., level of effort) than in performance itself. This is a point that has not been recognized in occupational stress research because the emphasis has clearly been on directly examining relations between stressors and performance (see Sullivan & Bhagat, 1992).

A third and final proposition is that of all of the antecedents of performance, stressors probably have the greatest impact on those that are influenced by *motivation*. It is unlikely, in most cases, that stressors would have a negative impact on antecedents such as declarative knowledge or procedural knowledge/skills (Campbell, 1990), because these are strongly influenced by innate ability. The same conclusion can also be drawn if one considers the antecedents of performance in Sternberg's (1994) model. For example, things such as abilities, thinking styles, personality, and values are relatively enduring characteristics of the individual. The overall point here is that stressors often impact performance (we will assume that this impact is not *always* negative) by influencing the *choices* employees make regarding where to direct their efforts, the level of effort to exert, and whether or not to utilize their innate abilities fully.

An important corollary to this third point is that stressors are most likely to have an impact on performance *dimensions* that are heavily influenced by motivation. In Campbell's (1990) model, which was discussed earlier, the dimensions of "demonstrating effort," "maintaining personal discipline," and "facilitating peer and team performance" would certainly fit this category. Organ's (1994) more general category of organizational citizenship behavior would also fit this definition. This again is a point that has largely been overlooked by occupational stress researchers. In fact, I know of only one study (Kruse, 1995) that has examined relations between job-related stressors and organizational citizenship behaviors. In this same vein, few occupational stress studies have examined relations between stressors and counterproductive behaviors (e.g., Spector, 1997b; Storms & Spector, 1987).

Although these three general propositions certainly do not constitute a comprehensive theory linking specific stressors with specific performance dimensions (Fried & Tiegs, 1995), they are certainly a step in the right direction. Furthermore, they may serve as a useful guide to researchers when choosing performance outcomes. They may also be useful to managers trying to ascertain whether job-related stressors may be contributing to an employee performance problem.

Complicating Factors

At this point, the reader has hopefully developed some appreciation for the complexity of job performance. Because of this complexity, there are a number of factors that come into play in attempting to document the relationship between stressors and job performance. In this section, four of the most important complicating factors are discussed: (a) the measurement of job performance, (b) restriction in the variability of job performance, (c) instability of job performance, and (d) the form of stressor-performance relations.

Measurement of Job Performance

Because job performance is defined as behavior, it is quite rare that job performance is measured directly. More typically, what is measured is the *result* of job performance or some *external assessment* of job performance. According to Murphy (1989), there are eight different ways in which performance can be assessed (paper/pencil tests, job skills tests, on-site hands-on testing, off-site hands-on testing, high-fidelity simulations, symbolic simulations, task ratings, and global ratings). By far the two most common of the performance assessment methods described by Murphy are ratings of employees' performance on specific tasks and ratings of overall performance on the job.

Because the literature on performance rating is vast (e.g., Landy & Farr, 1980; Murphy & Cleveland, 1990), it will not be reviewed in detail here. Two general points, however, can be made. First, there are many potential sources of error in performance ratings. For example, a rater may not have an adequate opportunity to observe performance, ratings may be biased by the degree to which the rater likes or dislikes the ratee, or raters may systematically use different performance standards. These are just three of many potential sources of error. Such errors ultimately mask meaningful differences in actual job performance and thus may weaken the relationship between stressors and job performance.

A second point is that steps *can* be taken to reduce error in performance ratings. For example, rater training has been shown to increase accuracy in performance ratings (Pulakos, 1984). Given the problems with performance ratings, it is often tempting to seek more "objective" performance measures, such as output produced or sales commissions. Unfortunately, these supposedly more objective performance measures also may have serious flaws. The most obvious of these is that, in many cases, they are really measures of *effectiveness* rather than of actual job performance (Campbell, 1990). Another disadvantage is that employees may lack control over these performance indicators. For example, even a very skilled real estate salesperson would probably not sell many houses if the mortgage interest rate rose to 20%.

Restriction in the Variability of Job Performance

A second complicating factor in assessing the relation between stressors and job performance is low variability in job performance. For a variety of reasons, the variability in performance levels in many organizations is often restricted. In order to understand this phenomenon, it is useful to contrast what might be called *artifactual* restriction in performance variability with *true* restriction. Artifactual restriction in performance variability results from things such as errors in performance ratings. That is, even though there may be true differences among employees in levels of job performance, there may be so much error in performance ratings that all employees receive very similar ratings. True restriction in performance variability, on the other hand, occurs when performance ratings are relatively accurate but there is a lack of meaningful variation in actual job performance. In this section, true range restriction is discussed.

According to Peters and O'Connor (1988), there are four reasons why individual variation in performance may be restricted. First, organizations simply may have very low performance standards. If organizations do not expect much, this will tend to discourage high levels of performance. Instead, many employees will gravitate toward "minimally acceptable" levels of performance. The end result of this process is often a great reduction in the variability of performance.

A second factor, which is related to low performance standards, is that organizations vary in the degree to which they value individual job performance. Of course, top managers in most organizations *say* they value high levels of job performance. In reality, however, many organizations either do not adequately recognize the contributions of those who perform well, or they tolerate individuals who consistently perform at a very low level. In some cases, low levels of performance are even inadvertently *rewarded*. For example, I once worked in a department in which the most incompetent member was promoted to a higher-paying job in another department within the company. The reason for this apparently illogical action, I was told later, was that the manager of my department saw this as a way to be rid of the marginal employee. Such actions may ultimately reduce job performance to the lowest common denominator, with the end result being a reduction in performance variability.

A third factor restricting the variability in performance is the degree to which organizations will excuse employees for low levels of performance. This, again, is related to low performance standards, but in practice it operates somewhat differently. According to Peters and O'Connor (1988), organizations may develop what they describe as a "culture of justification" (p. 117). That is, employees are routinely allowed to "explain away" instances of poor performance. The impact of such a culture, one would assume, would again be to take away the incentive to perform well and thereby restrict performance to mediocre levels.

A final cause of restriction in performance variability, according to Peters and O'Connor (1988), is organizational variation in resources. Having limited resources would, of course, introduce situational constraints (Peters & O'Connor, 1980). On the other hand, if organizational resources are extremely *plentiful,* this may also reduce the variability in performance. In this case, however, everyone in an organization may perform up to his or her full potential and, as a result, the variability in performance will be restricted.

A somewhat different explanation as to why the variation in actual performance levels may be restricted is that organizations do not hire randomly. According to Johns (1991), in most organizations employees must pass through relatively rigorous screening processes before they are hired. As a result, the variation in skill and ability level among employees may be quite restricted, which may ultimately restrict the variability in job performance. Of course, one must remember that organizations are not always able to hire the most capable applicants (Murphy, 1986). Nevertheless, it is still likely that selection procedures ultimately do serve to create some uniformity in actual performance levels.

Regardless of the cause, a lack of variability in job performance will often weaken relations with stressors. Perhaps the best way to tackle this problem is simply to put more thought into the selection of performance criterion measures. There are undoubtedly differences among performance measures in the degree to which variability is restricted. As an example, organizational citizenship behavior is probably impacted less by many of the factors described above compared to measures of in-role performance.

Instability of Job Performance

There has been considerable debate over the years concerning the relative stability of performance criterion measures (e.g., Ackerman, 1989; Austin, Humphreys, & Hulin, 1989; Barrett, Caldwell, & Alexander, 1985; Henry & Hulin, 1987, 1989). Specifically, some have claimed that performance is relatively stable over time, while others have argued that it is more dynamic. The weight of the evidence seems to support the position that performance criteria are dynamic. For example, in a study of sewing machine operators, Deadrick and Madigan (1990)

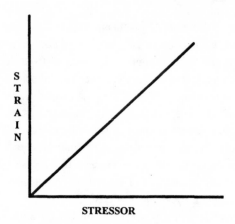

Figure 3.2. A Graphic Representation of a Linear Relationship Between a Stressor and a Strain

found that performance was quite stable when the time interval was very short. However, the correlation between performance at one point in time and performance 23 weeks later was considerably weaker. This suggests that, due to a variety of factors, employee performance may fluctuate somewhat over time.

What is the impact of performance instability on stressor-performance relations? One logical possibility is that the relations between stressors and performance may also be unstable. This possibility will be examined in more depth in Chapter 5, as we explore the impact of job experience on stressor-performance relationships. Unfortunately, because data in most occupational stress studies are collected at only one point in time, there is very little empirical evidence available to address this issue.

The Form of Stressor-Performance Relations

Most statistical techniques used in the organizational sciences are based on the assumption that the form of relationships between variables is *linear* (e.g., Nunnally & Bernstein, 1994). All this means is that if you plotted the relationship between two variables, the form of this plot would resemble a straight line (see Figure 3.2 for a simple illustration). For many research domains, the assumption of linearity is quite viable.

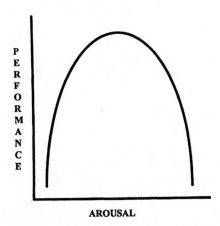

AROUSAL

Figure 3.3. A Graphic Representation of the Yerkes-Dodson Law

When studying the relationship between stressors and performance, however, this assumption may be less viable. Long ago, Yerkes and Dodson (1908) proposed what has come to be known as the Yerkes-Dodson Law. This law simply states that the relationship between a person's level of physiological arousal and performance can be described in terms of an inverted U-shaped function (see Figure 3.3). What this means is that as arousal increases, performance initially improves. After this initial improvement, performance will increase to an optimal level and then deteriorate as arousal becomes too great. More recent work on this issue has shown that as task complexity increases, the optimal level of performance will be reached sooner than the point initially proposed by Yerkes and Dodson (Broadbent, 1971; Easterbrook, 1959; Kahneman, 1973).

The relevance of the Yerkes-Dodson Law to the relationship between stressors and performance seems quite obvious, because stressors may increase physiological arousal (Ganster & Schaubroeck, 1991b). Unfortunately, very little nonlaboratory research has been conducted with the idea that the relation between job-related stressors and performance resembles an inverted U-shaped curve. Therefore, in most occupational stress studies, no tests for nonlinear effects are conducted. One notable exception was a recent study by Xie and Johns (1995), which found that relations between job complexity (which is closely related to stress) and mental health outcomes was consistent with the Yerkes-Dodson Law. In the future, more occupational stress researchers need to investigate this possibility when examining performance as an outcome.

Conclusion

The general purpose of this chapter was to facilitate an understanding of job performance. This is important because it is hard to predict something that one does not understand. There are two major points, in particular, to be gleaned from this chapter. The first is that investigating the relationship between stressors and job performance is just another form of performance prediction. As a result, I was able to draw on literature (e.g., Campbell, 1990; Murphy, 1994) that examines performance prediction largely in the context of personnel selection.

A second point is that job performance is a *complex, multidimensional* variable that is affected by many things. Given this complexity, it would seem essential in the investigation of stressor-performance relations to (a) specify exactly what one *means* by job performance and (b) develop hypotheses about stressors and specific performance dimensions. Unfortunately, occupational stress researchers have largely treated job performance as a simple, unitary concept (Fried & Tiegs, 1995).

4

The Evidence

Empirical Research on Stressors and Job Performance

Now that the reader has a better understanding of both job-related stressors and job performance, it is time to examine the relationship between these two variables. To that end, this chapter will summarize empirical research that has examined the relationship between stressors and job performance. It will be organized according to the job-related stressors that were covered in Chapter 2, in order to maintain consistency. In addition, several studies have examined the performance-related impact of stressors that were not covered in Chapter 2. These are summarized in a separate section.

Perhaps the biggest dilemma in preparing this chapter was deciding which studies to include and which not to include. In making this decision, a rather broad definition of job performance was used. That is, studies are certainly included that have examined the impact of stressors on traditional performance indicators such as supervisory ratings. On the other hand, studies are also included that have examined performance-related behaviors that are not typically assessed in performance reviews (e.g., extra-role behaviors, counterproductive behaviors). This was done largely to be consistent with the point made in Chapter 3 regarding the complexity of job performance and the relevance of different types of performance to workplace stressors.

Role Stressors

Role Conflict and Role Ambiguity

As stated in Chapter 2, considerable occupational stress research has examined the impact of role stressors. This is especially true of role conflict and role ambiguity. Because of this large volume of research, there have been attempts to summarize the impact of role conflict and role ambiguity statistically, using a technique known as *meta-analysis*. Meta-analysis is simply a statistical technique used to combine the findings from several studies. It basically involves averaging the correlations from different studies while adjusting for differences between studies in sample size, scale reliability, and range restriction (the interested reader is referred to Hunter & Schmidt, 1990, or Rosenthal, 1991, for more technical discussions of meta-analysis).

The most widely cited meta-analysis of the impact of role conflict and role ambiguity was conducted by Jackson and Schuler (1985). These researchers examined nearly 100 studies conducted between 1970 and 1982. From these studies, correlations between role stressors and number of outcomes were extracted. In the majority of studies that assessed performance outcomes, ratings by others (e.g., supervisors or peers) were used. Some studies, however, included either self-assessments or more objective performance indicators (e.g., sales volume, profits, number of publications).

The findings from the Jackson and Schuler study indicated that neither of these role stressors was strongly correlated with performance ratings from supervisors or peers (role conflict = −.11; role ambiguity = −.12). Correlations were also very weak when performance was measured objectively (role conflict = −.02; role ambiguity = −.10). When performance was measured through self-ratings, role conflict was still unrelated to performance (−.03). Role ambiguity, however, was more strongly correlated with self-assessments (−.37) compared to the other two performance measures. In considering the magnitude of these average correlations, it is important to note that Jackson and Schuler found substantial variation in correlations between studies. This suggests the possibility that the relationship between role stressors and performance may be affected by other variables. This issue will be examined in more depth in Chapter 5.

Since Jackson and Schuler's (1985) study, two other meta-analyses have provided additional insight into the relationship between these role stressors and performance. For example, Abramis (1994) summarized the relationship between role ambiguity and performance in 11 separate studies covering the period from 1967 to 1990. In doing so, he included some studies that were not examined in the Jackson and Schuler meta-analysis. Like Jackson and Schuler, Abramis examined differences in the relationship between role ambiguity and performance, based on the source of the performance rating (e.g., self, peer, or supervisor). No studies were included in which performance was assessed though objective indicators.

Abramis's (1994) results were quite similar to Jackson and Schuler's with respect to role ambiguity. Specifically, the average correlation between role ambiguity and performance rated by others was –.08, whereas role ambiguity was correlated –.24 with self-ratings. Also, like Jackson and Schuler, Abramis found noticeable variation in these correlations between studies.

The most recent meta-analytic investigation of the impact of role conflict and role ambiguity was conducted by Tubre, Sifferman, and Collins (1996). These authors summarized 43 correlations between role ambiguity and performance and 32 correlations between role conflict and performance. The years in which the studies from which these data were taken overlapped with the previously described meta-analyses. Unlike the previous meta-analyses, however, these authors statistically corrected the correlations for measurement error in the performance ratings (see Viswesvaran, Ones, & Schmidt, 1996). This is important because measurement error may artificially weaken the correlations between role stressors and performance ratings. Therefore, correcting correlations in this manner potentially provides a more accurate estimate of the relation between role stressors and performance.

The results of the Tubre et al. (1996) meta-analysis are consistent with both Jackson and Schuler (1985) and Abramis (1994). Specifically, role ambiguity was generally more strongly correlated with performance than was role conflict. Furthermore, the strongest correlation was between role ambiguity and self-rated performance, –.25, a figure that is quite similar to both previously described meta-analyses. An additional similarity is that there was again considerable variation among studies in the magnitude of the correlations.

Although the results of these three meta-analyses are certainly useful, all summarize studies that have defined performance in rather narrow terms. That is, in most of the studies summarized, "performance" is measured in terms of in-role, largely nonsupervisory tasks. A recent study by Fried and Tiegs (1995) assessed the impact of role conflict and ambiguity on the performance of a typical supervisory task, namely rating subordinate performance. These authors predicted that supervisors experiencing high levels of role conflict would be more likely to inflate subordinates' performance ratings, compared to those who were not. Inflating these ratings, it was reasoned, would make it easier for supervisors to cope with conflicting role demands because they would not have to justify low ratings to subordinates. No relationship between role ambiguity and performance ratings was predicted.

Data from three supervisory samples supported the hypothesized relationship between role conflict and inflation of performance ratings. Specifically, in two of these samples, role conflict was correlated with *self-reported* inflation of ratings. Somewhat unexpectedly, role ambiguity was also correlated with supervisors' reports in one of these samples. In the third sample, Fried and Tiegs (1995) examined the *actual* distribution of ratings and found role conflict to be strongly related to the tendency to give more lenient performance ratings.

This study obviously has important implications for performance appraisal. It is also important in the present context because it assessed the impact of role stressors on one aspect of managerial job performance, namely performance rating, which has been largely ignored by occupational stress researchers. Perhaps more important, their findings show quite clearly that hypotheses need to be stated in terms of specific stressors and specific dimensions of job performance. It is certainly more informative to predict that, "Role conflict will lead to inflated performance ratings" than simply to say, "Role conflict will have a negative impact on managerial performance." It is hoped that more investigations of stressor-performance relations will be conducted in this manner.

In summary, the weight of the evidence suggests that neither role conflict nor role ambiguity is strongly related to job performance. Of the two, however, role ambiguity seems to impact performance more strongly than role conflict. Another consistent finding from the three meta-analyses reviewed is that role ambiguity was most strongly related to self-rated performance, compared to either ratings from other sources or objective measures. This may be due to methodological biases, because both measures are being obtained from the same source (Spector, 1994). Given the problems with performance ratings noted in the previous chapter, however, it may also be due to the fact that supervisor and peer ratings are somewhat deficient indicators of actual performance (Mabe & West, 1982; Murphy & Cleveland, 1990). One final point regarding this issue is that employee *percep-*

tions of performance are important. Even if role ambiguity does not impair actual performance, it still may have negative performance implications if it causes employees to feel that their performance is lacking. Such employees may lose confidence (Bandura, 1997), which may ultimately lead to actual performance decrements in the future.

Role Overload

Compared to role conflict and role ambiguity, there has been relatively little research on role overload. This is unfortunate because, in recent years, many organizations have undergone changes (e.g., downsizing, mergers and acquisitions) that may lead to overload (Hogan & Overmeyer-Day, 1994; Kozlowski et al., 1993). One exception is a study in which Jamal (1984) investigated the relationship between role overload and supervisory performance ratings among a sample of nurses in several Canadian hospitals. An interesting feature of this investigation was that supervisors rated the nurses on three separate dimensions of performance—overall job performance, job motivation, and the level of patient care provided. This allowed the assessment of whether role overload has different effects on different aspects of job performance.

The results of Jamal's (1984) study indicated that role overload was negatively correlated with all three measures of job performance (i.e., high role overload was associated with lower levels of performance). Furthermore, the magnitude of these correlations (overall performance = –.33; job motivation = –.27; patient care = –.31) was quite similar. This is not surprising, because these three performance dimensions were strongly interrelated.

In a subsequent investigation, Jamal (1985) examined the correlation between role overload and supervisory performance ratings among a sample of mid-level managers and a sample of blue-collar workers. Both samples of employees were employed by the same organization. As in his previous study, Jamal included ratings of multiple performance dimensions. In this case, both samples of employees were rated by supervisors in terms of quality of performance, quantity of performance, and effort exerted.

The results of this study indicated that, in both samples, high levels of role overload were associated with decrements in both the quality and quantity of performance. These correlations, however, were somewhat weaker than those reported for the nursing sample. For example, correlations between role overload and quality of performance were –.19 for the managerial sample and –.14 for the blue-collar sample, respectively. For performance quantity, the correlations were −.11 for the managerial sample and −.18 for the blue-collar sample, respectively.

One surprising finding from the Jamal (1985) study was that, in both samples, role overload was unrelated to ratings of effort exerted. Given the nature of role overload, it seems plausible that an employee who is overloaded would exert greater effort than an employee who is not, in order to keep up. On the other hand, if one were extremely overloaded, one way to cope would simply be to give up and reduce one's effort (e.g., Seligman, 1975). If some employees in this study used the first approach and some used the latter, this may have effectively "washed out" the relationship between role overload and effort exerted.

The most recent study that has investigated the performance-related effects of role overload was conducted by Beehr et al. (1997). In this case, the sample consisted of college students who were employed for the summer selling children's books door to door. The study differs from Jamal's (1984, 1985) previous investigations of role overload in that performance was not assessed through supervisory ratings. Rather, these investigators measured performance in terms of the number of sales demonstrations conducted and the dollar value of sales generated during the summer.

The results of the Beehr et al. (1997) study indicated that role overload was not correlated with either performance measure. However, when the effects of other types of stressors were controlled (using multiple regression analysis; see Cohen & Cohen, 1983), role overload was actually positively related to dollar value of sales. Although this finding may simply be due to the fact that role overload was correlated with other stressors examined in this study (this is known as a "suppressor effect"; Nunnally & Bernstein, 1994), it may also have substantive implications. Specifically, Beehr et al. stated that employees who are experiencing the greatest overload may also be achieving the highest levels of performance. This may be particularly true, given the nature of the job held by employees in this sample. In a sales position, being overloaded may simply mean that there is a high demand for the product(s) one is selling. The more general point to be gleaned from Beehr et al. is that performance-related effects may be quite specific to the stressor and the performance dimension under investigation.

In summary, based on rather limited evidence, it appears that role overload may have a negative effect on performance. In some cases, however, feelings of being overloaded may accompany high levels of performance. The key, in future investigations of this stressor, is to pay close attention to the specific performance dimension(s) being measured.

Workload

As was shown in Chapter 2, workload can be measured in a variety of ways. For example, occupational stress researchers have measured workload in terms of number of employee reports of hours worked (Spector et al., 1988), employees' perceptions of workload (Jex & Gudanowski, 1992), and a variety of non-self-report indexes (e.g., Caplan & Jones, 1975). Research reviewed in this section will consider studies that have measured workload in each of these three ways.

During my search for evidence on the relationship between workload and job performance, it became clear that few occupational stress researchers have directly examined the performance-related effects of this stressor. Rather, most work has focused on the health-related effects of workload (e.g., Cooper & Marshall, 1976; Frankenhaeuser, 1979; Sparks, Cooper, Fried, & Shirom, 1997). The major finding from such studies has been that excessive workload is associated with health problems. Of course, poor health may also impair an employee's ability to perform and thus indirectly lead to performance decrements.

A small number of studies have directly examined the relationship between workload and job performance. For example, Spector et al. (1988) examined the relationship among three measures of workload (employee perceptions, work hours, and number of people worked for) and supervisory ratings of performance among a sample of female clerical employees. A unique feature of this study was that, in addition to providing performance ratings, supervisors also rated the level of workload (and several other stressors) of each of these employees. Thus, these researchers were able to examine the impact of workload measured both from the point of view of job incumbents and from the point of view of supervisors.

The results of this study indicated that none of the self-reported workload measures was correlated with performance. Supervisor reports of work hours and number of people worked for were unrelated to performance as well. Interestingly, though, supervisor reports of employees' perceptions of workload were positively correlated with performance (.28). Employees who were perceived by supervisors as having heavier workloads were also rated as having higher levels of performance.

There are several ways to interpret the findings from the Spector et al. (1988) study. For instance, it may simply be that employees who had heavier workloads were accomplishing more and, hence, received higher performance ratings (Beehr, 1976; Beehr et al., 1997). It is also possible, given the design of this study, that supervisors may have made inferences about employees' workload based on performance levels. Supervisors may have assumed that employees who were performing well also had higher levels of workload.

These findings may also have been due to the fact that supervisors and job incumbents had differing views of incumbents' levels of workload. Specifically, the correlation between incumbent and supervisor reports of perceived workload was .49, which means that the shared variation in these ratings was 25% (this is obtained by squaring the correlation coefficient). Thus, an employee may view his or her workload differently than others (e.g., coworkers, supervisor, spouse). This underscores the importance of obtaining measures of employees workload from multiple data sources.

A final explanation for the findings reported by Spector et al. (1988) is that perhaps the level of workload reported by this sample was not extreme enough to lead to performance decrements. As described in Chapter 3, the Yerkes-Dodson Law states that the relation between arousal and performance can be described as an inverted U. Assuming that arousal is positively related to workload, arousal may be positively related to performance up to a certain point. After this point, however, higher levels of workload may lead to performance decrements.

Thus, despite the contribution of the Spector et al. (1988) study, it still leaves unanswered two important questions regarding the performance-related effects of workload. First, if workload is sometimes positively related to performance, why is it generally associated with poor health (Sparks et al., 1997)? Second, if extreme levels of workload do lead to performance decrements, what is (are) the mechanism(s) by which this occurs?

Both of these issues were addressed in a literature review by Spurgeon and Harrington (1989) that examined the relationship between workload and both performance and health among junior hospital physicians. Much of the research in this review comes from studies conducted in the United Kingdom that have examined the performance and health-related effects of the excessive work hours that often accompany medical training. An obvious concern is that excessive work hours may lead to mistakes that negatively impact the quality of patient care.

One conclusion from this review is that excessive work hours do lead to both mental and physical health problems, primarily due to sleep deprivation. With regard to performance, however, the impact of work hours and sleep deprivation is more complex. For example, Spurgeon and Harrington (1989) cite several studies showing that performance on a number of tasks declines with increasing sleep deprivation (e.g., Friedman, Bigger, & Kornfield, 1971; Rechtscheffen & Kales, 1968). What these tasks have in common is that they require monitoring or constant attention (e.g., monitoring a patient's vital signs). According to Kjellberg (1977), lower levels of arousal caused by sleep loss will lead to poor performance on such tasks, because this impairs the ability to sustain attention for long periods of time.

Despite the potential negative effects of sleep deprivation, the performance-related impact is by no means inevitable. For example, it has been shown that the nature of the task one is performing may have an impact on the level of performance impairment. In general, when tasks are engaging and motivating, individuals may show smaller or little or no performance decrements as a result of sleep deprivation (e.g., Poulton, Hunt, Carpenter, & Edwards, 1978). It has also been shown that the effects of sleep loss may be cumulative (Webb & Levy, 1984). Thus, examining the relation between workload measures and performance at one point in time may not necessarily indicate a relation between these variables. Over time, though, performance may gradually decline.

Two studies conducted after Spurgeon and Harrington's (1989) review shed additional light on the impact of excessive workload among physicians. Using a sample of resident physicians from the United States, Jex et al. (1991) examined the relations between four self-reported workload measures (number of nights on call, sleep deprivation, working excessive hours, and number of changes in work schedules) and a composite measure of performance based on the frequency of a number of behaviors that may have affected performance (unexplained absences, making mistakes, missing deadlines, and conflict with hospital staff).

The results of this study indicated that all four workload measures were negatively correlated with this behavioral composite, suggesting that high levels of workload may have been associated with poorer performance in this group. The workload measure that was most strongly related was number of schedule changes. This finding is consistent with the literature on shiftwork regarding the negative impact of rotating shifts (Hurrell & Colligan, 1987). It also suggests that sheer number of hours may be a rather deficient indicator of workload.

It is somewhat risky to generalize the research on physicians to employees in other occupations. Despite this risk, there are a number of important points to be drawn from this literature. First, it appears that workload, at least as measured by hours, must be rather excessive in order to affect performance adversely. For example, according to Spurgeon and Harrington (1989), it is not unusual for junior physicians in the United Kingdom to work as many as 102 hours in a given week. Excessively long hours are also quite common during medical residency training in the United States (Butterfield, 1988). It is unlikely (though certainly not unheard of) that individuals in most occupations work that many hours, and thus the work performance of employees in most occupations is not seriously affected by sheer number of work hours.

A second point is that the most likely mechanism by which excessive work hours lead to performance decrements is loss of sleep. Obviously, it is quite possible that a person working an excessive number of hours, or working on a large number of projects, may be sleep deprived. On the other hand, depending on one's lifestyle, it may still be possible to obtain adequate amounts of sleep even during periods of excessive workload. Furthermore, even if one experiences a loss of sleep, there is evidence that the probability of impaired performance can be reduced by periods of intervening sleep (Bonnet, 1986).

A final point is that the impact of work hours (and perhaps other workload indexes) depends on the nature of the task(s) being performed by employees. As stated above, the literature on physicians suggests that excessive workloads are most likely to lead to performance decrements on tasks that may require sustained attention for long periods of time (e.g., "vigilance tasks"; Beatty, Adhern, & Katz, 1977). This is an important point when one considers that, as technology has changed over the years, the number of jobs requiring the performance of such tasks has increased considerably (Human Capital Initiative, 1993). Of course, another important point is that designing jobs so they are interesting and engaging (Griffin, 1991; Hackman & Oldham, 1980) may go a long way toward reducing potential performance decrements associated with workload.

Situational Constraints

Of all the stressors covered in this book, situational constraints are probably the most logically and directly related to job performance. That is, when organizational or job conditions make it more difficult for people to do their jobs, it is quite logical that job performance would suffer. Despite the logical relationship between situational constraints and job performance, empirical evidence for such a relationship is quite mixed. For example, Peters, O'Connor, and Rudolf (1980) found that situational constraints inhibited both the quantity and quality of performance of subjects performing a laboratory task (building three-dimensional models from standard Erector set parts). Subsequent laboratory studies have consistently supported this hypothesis (e.g., O'Connor, Peters, & Segovis, 1983; Peters, Fisher, & O'Connor, 1982). The implication of these laboratory studies is that if situational constraints are intentionally imposed in a relatively novel situation, task performance will likely decline.

In contrast to laboratory investigations, relations between situational constraints and job performance have been very inconsistent in field studies. O'Connor, Peters, Eulberg, and Watson (1984) found no relationship between situational constraints and performance within seven samples of Air Force personnel. On the other hand, O'Connor, Peters, Pooyan, et al. (1984) found that the constraints variable was correlated with performance among a sample of managers from a national convenience store chain. In this study, however, the correlation was only −.10.

Steel and Mento (1986) examined the relationship between situational constraints and performance in a sample of branch managers from a financial services company. This study is unique because these authors examined the impact of situational constraints on multiple performance indicators. Specifically, supervisor ratings and self-ratings of performance were supplemented with more objective performance indexes (e.g., loan growth, profitability of branches, and control of past due accounts). These authors also used a measure of situational constraints that was shorter than the Peters et al. (1980) scale that was used in previous studies.

The results of the Steel and Mento (1986) study indicated that the situational constraints measure was correlated with both supervisory ratings (−.36) and self-ratings of performance (−.31). Of the objective performance indexes, the constraints measure was correlated only with control of past due accounts (−.12). This suggests that situational constraints do in fact inhibit performance. However, because the only performance measures that were related to constraints were supervisory ratings and self-ratings, it is possible that ratings were biased by the raters' knowledge of the situational constraints of these employees. In one subsequent study, self-reported situational constraints were found to be weakly related (−.18) to performance ratings (Spector et al., 1988).

In reviewing the inconsistent results of field studies, Peters and O'Connor (1988) offer several reasons why constraints may be related to performance in some instances but unrelated in others. These authors make the important point that in order for situational constraints to inhibit performance, several conditions must be present. Specifically, job tasks must be sufficiently challenging, organizations must place a high value on job performance, and employees must not easily be able to make excuses for poor performance. The reality, according to Peters and O'Connor, is that in many instances, these assumptions simply are not tenable. They also point out that constraints will not have an impact on performance if resources are so plentiful as to eliminate constraints in the first place (see also the discussion in Chapter 3 of restriction in the variability of job performance).

Because organizational conditions may suppress the relationship between situational constraints and many indicators of performance, a key issue is the nature of the performance measure used. For example, Kruse (1995) argued that situational constraints may be only weakly related to performance because past studies have used measures of in-role performance. In contrast, performance measures that assess "extra-role" performance or organizational citizenship behaviors may be less impacted by those factors described by Peters and O'Connor (1988) because these behaviors, by definition, are more discretionary (Organ, 1994).

In order to test this proposition, Kruse (1995) examined the relationship between self-reported situational constraints and coworker ratings of five different forms of organizational citizenship behavior (altruism, sportsmanship, courtesy, civic virtue, and conscientiousness; Organ, 1994). *Altruism* is defined as helping others who are in need (e.g., helping a new employee log on to his or her computer). *Sportsmanship* is defined as refraining from complaining about minor problems and inconveniences (e.g., not complaining about occasional overtime work). *Courtesy* is defined as showing consideration for and tact toward others in the workplace (e.g., letting coworkers know where one can be reached). *Civic virtue* is defined as doing "extra" things on behalf of the organization (e.g., attending a company-sponsored community event). *Conscientiousness* is defined as being reliable and consistent in one's behavior (e.g., coming to work on time).

Using a sample consisting mainly of managerial/professional employees, the results indicated reports of situational constraints were correlated with sportsmanship (–.21), courtesy (–.27), and altruism (–.20). The constraints measure was unrelated to both civic virtue and conscientiousness. These results offer moderate support for the proposed relation between situational constraints and organizational citizenship behavior. Specifically, employees who perceive many situational constraints may be more likely to complain about small things, less likely to extend some forms of courtesy to coworkers, and perhaps may be less likely to offer assistance to others.

Unfortunately, the Kruse (1995) study does not answer the question of whether organizational citizenship behavior is a better performance indicator than in-role performance measures, because these were not directly compared. Also, when considering the magnitude of correlations reported in this study, these were not that much higher than correlations that have been reported between constraints and in-role performance (e.g., Peters & O'Connor, 1988). Unfortunately, this study is also somewhat limited because the sample size was rather small ($N = 100$).

Another form of job performance that may be related to situational constraints is *counterproductive behavior*. An employee may engage in counterproductive behavior in a number of ways: by being overtly rude to others, ignoring coworkers when they need assistance, complaining about very minor problems, refusing to do anything on behalf of the organization, and being unreliable. Counterproductive behavior may also take more extreme forms and include things such as sabotage, theft, and even physical assault (Spector, 1997b).

Several studies conducted over the years by Spector and his associates (e.g., Chen & Spector, 1992; Storms & Spector, 1987) have shown that situational constraints may lead to many forms of counterproductive behavior. For example, Chen and Spector (1992) found situational constraints to be correlated with interpersonal aggression (.31), hostility and complaining (.51), and theft (.18). Storms and Spector (1987) also reported correlations between situational constraints and counterproductive behaviors (e.g., aggression = −.36; sabotage = −.29; hostility and complaining = −.47). A limitation of both of these studies is that the counterproductive behaviors examined were self-reported. Nevertheless, situational constraints appear to be considerably more predictive of this type of behavior than more typical measures of job performance.

In considering the mechanism by which constraints lead to counterproductive behaviors, Spector (1996) notes that a key variable may be employee perceptions of control. Specifically, employees most likely to respond to situational constraints in counterproductive ways are those who believe they have little control over constraints. Employees who believe they do have control may respond more productively by trying to do something about the constraints (e.g., asking for better equipment, seeking clarification if job-related information is inadequate). It is also worth noting that some people may simply be more predisposed to counterproductive behavior than others (Ones, Viswesvaran, & Schmidt, 1993), regardless of the level of situational constraints. This is particularly true for extreme antisocial forms of counterproductive behavior.

A somewhat different explanation for the inconsistent relations between constraints and performance is offered in a recent study by Villanova (1996). This author argued that weak relations between situational constraints and performance may be due to the fact that constraints and performance often represent different levels of specificity. For example, a constraints measure may ask an employee to rate the extent to which certain general organizational conditions (e.g., lack of information) make it difficult to accomplish his or her job tasks. Performance measures, on the other hand, typically assess employee proficiency at a much greater level of specificity (e.g., providing high-quality service to customers).

Villanova also argues that, depending on the setting and job, some constraints (e.g., inadequate information) may have a greater impact on performance than others. This is an important point because typically when constraints are measured (e.g., Peters et al., 1980), responses to individual items (which represent specific constraints) are summed to form a composite index of the level of constraints.

To explore each of these two possibilities, Villanova (1996) examined relations between constraints and performance among students enrolled in a college-level mathematics course. The major finding from this study was that a measure that assessed constraints specific to the mathematics course predicted performance (semester grades) better than a measure that assessed factors that constrain academic performance in general. This study also showed that different types of constraints exhibited different relations with performance. For example, lack of time availability was most strongly correlated with semester grades (−.32), whereas lack of budgetary support was most weakly related (.06).

The overall lesson to be learned from this study is that occupational stress researchers must consider level of specificity when examining the relation between situational constraints and performance. In addition, all constraints are not equal in terms of their effect on performance. Perhaps most important, the study suggests that we still have much to learn about the manner in which situational constraints impact performance.

Perceived Control

As stated in Chapter 2, perceived control can be manifested in a number of ways in organizations. Two of the most common are through employees' level of job autonomy and the degree to which employees participate in decision making. Fortunately, considerable research has been done on both autonomy and participation. As a result, meta-analyses exist that summarize the impact of each on job performance. Results from two of these are described below.

The most widely cited meta-analysis that has assessed the relation between autonomy and job performance was performed by Fried and Ferris (1987). Based on eight samples of employees taken from studies conducted between 1975 and 1984, it was found that there was a positive correlation between autonomy and job performance, though it was rather weak (.18). That is, high levels of autonomy (which may indicate perceived control) were associated with high levels of job performance. By comparison, the correlation between autonomy and growth satisfaction was considerably larger (.71). These results suggest that although employees seem to *like* having job autonomy and are dissatisfied when they do not have it, the impact of job autonomy on performance seems to be much weaker.

A meta-analysis performed by Spector (1986) assessed the impact of job autonomy but also included studies that have investigated the impact of participation in decision making, another manifestation of perceived control. This meta-analysis was based on 101 samples of employees taken from 88 studies conducted between 1980 and 1985. The results showed that perceived control (as measured by both autonomy and participation) was correlated with job performance (.25). Furthermore, correlations did not seem to differ depending on whether perceived control was assessed through job autonomy (.26) or participation in decision making (.23). These findings are consistent with Fried and Ferris (1987), although the correlation between autonomy and job performance reported by Spector (1986) was a bit larger. Like Fried and Ferris, Spector found that perceived control was more strongly correlated with various forms of job satisfaction than it was with performance.

An important issue that has been examined and debated in more recent participation research is whether the specific *form* of participation makes a difference. For example, in a recent meta-analysis, Wagner (1994) found that the relationship between participation and performance was not influenced by the type of participation (e.g., formal vs. informal; short-term vs. long-term). This study, however, has met with rather strong criticism by some due to Wagner's rather narrow definition of participation (Cotton, 1995) and the statistical procedures used in some of the analyses (Sagie, 1995).

In considering all of the results discussed above, two points must be kept in mind. First, the vast majority of studies that were included in these meta-analyses assessed performance via supervisory ratings. Furthermore, in most cases these ratings assessed overall effectiveness. Thus, none of these meta-analyses assesses whether the effects of perceived control differ depending on the nature of the performance dimensions or the source of the ratings. The issue of rating source, in particular, may be important. For example, Wagner and Gooding (1987) found that participation was much more strongly related to self-rated performance than it was to performance ratings from other sources. This finding was supported in a more recent study of Canadian hospital employees in which Fisher (1995) found that participative decision making was more strongly related to self-rated performance (.30) than it was to either supervisory-rated performance (.18) or number of promotions (.20).

Second, the causal direction represented by the relationship between perceived control and performance is unclear. In models of occupational stress (see

Chapter 2), it is assumed that stressful job conditions lead to outcomes such as poor performance. With perceived control, however, it is certainly possible that the direction of causality could be the reverse. For example, a supervisor may be reluctant to give poorly performing employees much discretion over how to do their jobs, due to lack of trust (Dansereau, Graen, & Hagan, 1975; Yukl, 1992). For the same reason, it is unlikely that the supervisor would solicit the input of such persons when decisions are made. Unfortunately, in most studies, information regarding perceived control and job performance is collected at the same time, so it is difficult to assess causality empirically. This issue definitely needs to be addressed in future research.

In summary, a lack of perceived control seems to have a negative effect on performance. The magnitude of this effect, however, does not appear to be large. It is more likely that a lack of perceived control leads to negative feelings about the job, which perhaps leads employees to withdraw psychologically (Spector, 1986). Whether such withdrawal ultimately leads to performance decrements remains an unanswered question at present.

Interpersonal Conflict

Compared to the other stressors discussed to this point, less research has been conducted on the effects of interpersonal conflict. Nevertheless, some empirical evidence (and no doubt the day-to-day experience of many readers) suggests that this is an important source of stress in the workplace (e.g., Keenan & Newton, 1985).

Despite the lack of attention paid to interpersonal conflict, there is evidence that it may have an adverse effect on a variety of performance indexes. For example, Barnes, Potter, and Fiedler (1983) conducted two studies that investigated the impact of interpersonal conflict from a number of sources (peers, instructors, company officers, and parents) on the academic performance of cadets attending the U.S. Coast Guard Academy.

In the first of these studies, none of the four interpersonal conflict measures was related to academic performance, as measured by grade point average. In the second study, however, interpersonal conflict with parents and instructors was associated with lower levels of academic performance (−.29 and −.32, respectively). The implications of this study are rather interesting. The authors suggest that interpersonal conflict (and perhaps other stressors as well) may have a negative impact on certain aspects of cognitive functioning (e.g., attentional focus, creative thinking) that, in turn, may lead to actual performance decrements. This conclusion is particularly relevant for this study because academic performance is primarily a cognitive task. Also, one would assume that serious interpersonal conflicts in the workplace can be very distracting.

Despite the important implications of the Barnes et al. (1983) study, very little subsequent research has investigated the impact of interpersonal conflict on performance. One exception is a previously described study by Spector et al. (1988) that investigated the relation between interpersonal conflict and performance ratings among a sample of university clerical employees. This study found that interpersonal conflict was unrelated to performance.

In a more recent study, Chen and Spector (1992) investigated the relation between interpersonal conflict and number of counterproductive behaviors in the workplace. Their study is interesting because it expands the "criterion space" beyond more typically used measures of job performance. Basing their work on a sample of employees from 14 different organizations, these investigators found that interpersonal conflict was in fact associated with counterproductive behaviors. For example, reports of high levels of interpersonal conflict were positively associated with reports of sabotage (.34), interpersonal aggression and hostility (.49), and theft (.16). Interpersonal conflict was not correlated with reports of substance use in the workplace, however.

This study suggests that interpersonal conflict (like situational constraints) may have a negative impact on organizations because of its relation to counterproductive behaviors. Furthermore, depending on the nature of the counterproductive behavior, the impact on an organization can be extremely negative. For example, Kuhn (1988) reported that financial losses in the United States due to counterproductive behaviors were as much as $50 billion in 1986 and that this was rising. Given that such behaviors are not typically assessed during performance reviews, it is very easy to conclude that interpersonal conflict, and perhaps other stressors, has no impact on performance.

As previously discussed in the section on situational constraints, Chen and Spector's (1992) findings must be interpreted with caution due to the fact that all variables were self-reported. It was also pointed out that counterproductive behaviors may also be influenced by dispositional factors. This point is important because dispositional factors that may predispose one toward counterproductive behavior may also increase the propensity for interpersonal conflict. According to Spector (1997b), individuals who are likely to engage in counterproductive behaviors tend to be frustrated with work, impulsive, hostile toward authority, alienated, and insensitive toward others. It is not difficult to imagine that such characteristics may also lead to interpersonal conflicts with coworkers. Future research investigating interpersonal conflict and counterproductive behavior should assess the degree to which this relation is due to dispositional factors. Such research would prove to be not only theoretically meaningful, but it may also have important practical implications for organizations trying to reduce various forms of employee counterproductivity.

In summary, the relation between interpersonal conflict and job performance is clearly underresearched. Based on very limited findings, it appears that interpersonal conflict may have a negative impact on the performance of employees' job duties due to its negative impact on cognitive functioning. The greatest impact of interpersonal impact, though, may be its association with counterproductive behaviors. This relation, however, needs considerably more research before definitive conclusions can be drawn.

Acute Stressors

Up to this point, the stressors that have been covered are considered "chronic" because they are more or less a constant part of an employee's job or work environment (Beehr & Newman, 1978). Most occupational stress research has in fact assessed the impact of chronic stressors (see Jex & Beehr, 1991, for a review). Fortunately, over the years a limited number of studies have assessed the impact of stressors that are more acute or episodic in nature. Studies that have assessed the impact of these stressors on job performance are reviewed below.

Nowack and Hanson (1983) examined the relationship between discrete stressful life events and both burnout and job performance among a sample of college students performing the job of Resident Assistant in dormitories. Interestingly, performance ratings in this study were provided by the students residing in the dormitories. This represents a departure from supervisory ratings, which are more typically used to measure job performance.

The results of this study indicated that frequency of stressful life events was not correlated with job performance. However, in a regression analysis, frequency of life events was related to job performance after controlling for the effects of depersonalization (a dimension of burnout) and personality. Taken together, these results suggest that employees who are experiencing many major life changes may exhibit lower levels of performance. These results must be interpreted cautiously, though, because of the small sample size ($N = 37$) and the fact that these were student employees.

Much stronger evidence for the effects of acute stressors on performance was provided by Motowidlo, Packard, and Manning (1986) in a study of hospital nurses. These investigators developed a measure of stressful events that were specific to the nursing profession (e.g., "A doctor is verbally abusive toward you"; "A patient criticizes your nursing care"). This is an improvement over the Nowack and Hanson (1983) study because it is likely that job-related stressful events are more relevant to job performance than are general stressful life events (e.g., Bhagat, McQuaid, Lindholm, & Segovis, 1985). Furthermore, in measuring these stressful job events, Motowidlo et al. asked nurses to rate not only the *frequency* but also the *intensity* of the events. This is also important because it is possible that although a particular stressful event does not occur very frequently, it may nevertheless have a very negative impact on performance due to its intensity.

Perhaps the major strength of the Motowidlo et al. (1986) study was in the measurement of job performance. Unlike most studies that have assessed job performance in terms of overall effectiveness, these investigators assessed multiple dimensions of performance. More specifically, they obtained supervisory ratings of nurses' performance on the following performance dimensions: composure, quality of patient care, tolerance with patients, warmth toward other nurses, tolerance with nurses and doctors, interpersonal effectiveness, and cognitive/emotional effectiveness. Assessing these eight different dimensions allows us to determine whether stressors have a different impact on different aspects of performance. As previously stated, this is probably the biggest gap in our understanding of the relation between job stress and job performance (cf. Fried & Tiegs, 1995).

The results of the Motowidlo et al. (1986) study showed that both frequency and intensity of stressful job events were related to job performance. Specifically, frequency of stressful job events was related to ratings of composure (–.22), warmth toward other nurses (–.17), and tolerance with nurses and doctors (–.27). Intensity of stressful events was related only to composure (–.22). The magnitude of these correlations is fairly consistent with other studies that have been discussed in this chapter, suggesting again that stressors have negative impact on job performance although this effect is not large. The study provides an additional contribution, however, because it suggests that stressful job events may have the strongest impact on interpersonal aspects of job performance.

An additional finding worth noting is that Motowidlo et al. (1986) found evidence that stressors may not have a *direct* impact on job performance. Specifically, their data suggested that stressors may initially lead to negative emotional states such as feelings of distress and depression. Such emotional states, in turn, may lead to performance decrements. Another way to explain this process is to say that negative emotional states may *mediate* the relations between job-related stressors and performance. Thus far, the issue of mediation has been intentionally avoided in order to facilitate the clarity of presentation. This will be discussed, however, at the end of this chapter because it explains, at least in part, the small correlations that are generally found between job stressors and performance.

Building on the work of Motowidlo et al. (1986), Beehr et al. (1997) examined the relationship between stressful job events and the performance of sales personnel. As was previously described, participants in the study were college students who were employed for the summer selling children's books door to door. Like Motowidlo et al., these investigators developed measures of stressful job events that were specific to door-to-door sales (e.g., "Having the door slammed in their face"; "Receiving a check that bounced"). Participants were simply asked to rate the frequency with which each of these events occurred during the course of their summer employment. These researchers also developed a measure of more chronic stressful conditions that were specific to the door-to-door sales job (e.g., "Events such as baseball games and swim meets make it difficult to catch families at home"). Including this measure allows a comparison of the relative impact of acute and chronic stressors. Two job-specific performance criteria (number of sales presentations and dollar value of sales) were assessed.

Neither the acute nor the chronic measure was related to number of sales presentations. Both indexes, however, were related to dollar value of sales. Furthermore, the measure of chronic stressful job conditions (–.49) was more strongly related than was the measure of acute stressors (–.23). This suggests that conditions that are a constant part of one's job may have a greater negative impact than stressors that occur more episodically. These findings must be interpreted cautiously, though, because all data in this study were collected at the end of the summer. Because of this, participants' reports of stressors (acute and chronic) were obtained retrospectively. Therefore, it is possible that one's level of job performance may have colored perceptions of the job.

In summary, though only a few studies have investigated acute stressors, they show that these may have a negative impact on job performance. An important question that needs attention is the relative degree to which acute and chronic stressors impact performance, because most jobs include both (e.g., Allen & Jex, 1995).

Other Stressors

In this section, several studies are briefly discussed that have investigated chronic stressors other than those described in Chapter 2. In many cases, studies that fit into this category explore stressors that are specific to a particular occupation. For example, Borg, Riding, and Falzon (1991) examined the impact of occupational stress among primary school teachers in Malta using a scale that was designed specifically for teachers. This scale assessed stressful aspects of the job related to pupil misbehavior, time/resource difficulties, and professional recognition. They found that all of these stressors were associated with lowered career commitment, which presumably could lead to lower levels of performance.

Parker and Kulik (1995) took this same approach by examining the impact of job-specific stressors among a sample of registered nurses. In this case, a composite "Stress" measure was used by summing all of the items assessing stressful aspects of nursing work. This study showed that the composite stress measure was not correlated with either self-rated or supervisor-rated performance. Caution should be used when interpreting this study, however, because the sample size was rather low ($N = 73$). Thus, like many field-based studies, this simply may have lacked the statistical power necessary to detect a relationship between the stress measure and performance (see Mone, Mueller, & Mauland, 1996, for a more detailed discussion of this issue).

Kahn and Cooper (1990) developed a job-specific measure of stressors for a sample of dealers in financial markets in London. Unlike the Parker and Kulik (1995) study, the approach Kahn and Cooper took was to statistically sort these stressors into different dimensions. The specific stressors for these employees included "role conflict and changes," "taking risks and achieving high performance," "career and promotion prospects," "the challenge of management," "spending time on unproductive activities," "the effect of work on home life," "performance setbacks," "the office environment," "technological aspects of the job," "organizational culture and climate," and "lack of support and guidance from colleagues and superiors." This study, unfortunately, was not specifically focused on job performance. These authors did, however, measure alcohol intake (measured by number of drinks per week), a form of counterproductive behavior.

Interestingly, the only stressor that was correlated with alcohol intake was "performance setbacks," a variable that is very similar to situational constraints. This is consistent with previous research on counterproductive behavior (e.g., Spector, 1997b).

Another popular approach to measuring occupational stressors is basically to ask employees about both stressful job conditions and reactions to these conditions and to create a composite index labeled "Job Stress." As one example, Jones and Boye (1992) describe a number of studies in which they use an instrument called the Employee Attitude Inventory (London House, 1980). The Job Stress scale on this instrument contains items that assess negative perceptions of one's organization, negative emotional reactions, disgruntlement with work, work-family conflict, physical illness, and unprofessional or discourteous relations with customers and clients. Readers will note that many of these sample items from the job stressor scale are not "stressors" as defined in Chapter 2, yet this approach is still quite popular (see also Judge, Boudreau, & Bretz, 1994).

The focus of the research described by Jones and Boye (1992) was to identify the relationship between job stress and employee theft. Based on the results of five studies, these authors report a consistent relation between job stress and the dollar value of theft admissions. Moreover, the greatest theft admissions were found among employees who reported high levels of job stress *and* tolerant attitudes toward a variety of forms of dishonesty (also measured by the Employee Attitude Inventory). These results suggest again that job-related stressors may play a very important role in counterproductive behavior. Unfortunately, like most other studies that have investigated counterproductive behavior, the research cited by Jones and Boye is based largely on self-reports. Future research on counterproductive behavior that employs multiple methods is needed to support these findings.

A final approach to measuring stressors that does not fit in with the stressors discussed earlier in this chapter is to assess "fit" rather than specific stressful job conditions. This approach is based on the person-environment (P-E) fit approach to occupational stress (see Kristof, 1996), which was discussed briefly in Chapter 1. According to this approach, jobs become stressful when the demands of a job do not match the preferences or abilities of the job incumbent.

Basing their work on this notion, Villanova, Bernardin, Johnson, and Dahmus (1994) examined the relation between job compatibility and performance among a sample of motion picture theater personnel. Job compatibility was measured by the Job Compatibility Questionnaire (Bernardin, 1987), which measures respondent preferences for various aspects of a job. Performance was measured by supervisory ratings and an index of an employee's overall value to the organization. The value index was created by combining performance and retention.

The results of this study indicated, as expected, that job compatibility was positively related to both supervisory ratings (.22) and overall value to the organization (.41). In further analyses, however, the authors examined whether job compatibility would predict both performance ratings and overall value after controlling for both numerical and verbal ability. In these analyses, job compatibility was related only to overall value when these ability measures were controlled.

The P-E fit approach was also used in a study examining occupational stress among university teachers (Blix, Cruise, Mitchell, & Blix, 1994). In this case, the authors proposed that there was "misfit" when teachers perceived that the rewards offered by the job did not meet their needs. Respondents in this study also rated the level of stress they felt resulting from four roles that are typical of university faculty—teaching, research, professional activities, and service. Ratings from each of these activities were collapsed into a composite Work Stress index. Performance was assessed by asking respondents to rate the degree to which they felt their productivity had been affected by job-related stress. It was found that the perceived misfit between needs and rewards was very weakly related to respondents' perceptions that their productivity had been affected by job-related stressors (.13). As expected, greater misfit was associated with greater perceived performance problems. In contrast, the Work Stress index was quite strongly (.53) related to respondents' perceptions that their productivity had been negatively impacted by job stressors.

These findings, unfortunately, are rather difficult to interpret for two reasons. First, the "productivity" measure used in this study was not a measure of performance. Second, the misfit measure was created by taking the absolute difference between the measures of motivational style and perceptions of job rewards. Several authors (e.g., Cronbach & Furby, 1970; Edwards, 1994; Nunnally & Bernstein, 1994) have strongly advised against this practice because it increases measurement error. Such increased error may have contributed to the low correlation between misfit and productivity.

Conclusion

This chapter has summarized a tremendous amount of research investigating the relation between job stress and performance. The purpose of this final section is to "tie things together" by drawing a number of conclusions about this vast literature.

One conclusion that is fairly clear is that across all stressors and performance dimensions the relation between stress and job performance is not particularly strong. Why is this the case? One reason, frankly, is that there is considerable error in measuring job performance. This is perhaps most problematic when performance ratings are used, but all measures of performance are impacted by error. Also, stressors represent one of many factors that may impact job performance (e.g., Campbell, 1990; Sternberg, 1994). In fact, given the number of factors that do affect job performance (e.g., ability, motivation, luck), it is actually surprising that job-related stressors have any impact on job performance at all.

Given this initial conclusion, it is tempting to dismiss the relationship between job stressors and job performance as being unimportant. I feel that this would be a mistake for two reasons. First, there is considerable variation in relations between job stressors and performance. Such variation depends, to a large extent, on the nature of both the stressor and the performance measure employed. Second, from a more practical point of view, small effects may be very important. For example, if the job performance of a physician is even slightly affected by job-related stressors, this could have very important human consequences.

A second conclusion is that stressors seem to be more strongly related to performance criteria that fall outside of those dimensions that are typically assessed in performance reviews. Probably the best examples given are inflation of performance ratings (Fried & Tiegs, 1995), organizational citizenship (Kruse, 1995), and counterproductive behaviors (e.g., Jones & Boye, 1992). This strongly suggests that occupational stress researchers need to adopt a broad definition of performance in future investigations. For the practicing manager, this suggests that the performance-related impact of job stressors often may not be detected in performance reviews. Rather, the best indicator(s) that employee stress levels are too high may be employee refusal to help others, hostility and aggression, or other forms of counterproductive behavior.

A third conclusion is that, in many cases, the relationship between stressors and job performance may be *indirect*. That is, job-related stressors may induce negative emotional states that, in turn, impact performance. Another way to state this would be that emotional states *mediate* the relationship between job-related stressors and performance. This makes intuitive sense, although only a handful of studies have examined such mediational processes (e.g., Motowidlo et al., 1986). Furthermore, of the studies that have examined mediation, few have been strong tests because all data have been collected at the same point in time (i.e., they are "cross-sectional"). Nevertheless, it would be useful in future research to examine whether, and under what conditions, performance decrements are preceded by emotional processes.

A fourth and final conclusion is that the relationship between job stressors and performance is *complex*. That is, the performance-related impact of stressors may depend on a number of factors. Another way to state this would be that there may be a variety of factors that *moderate* the relationship between job-related stress and performance. Given that performance is largely due to an interaction between the person and the environment (see Chapter 3), this makes both intuitive and theoretical sense.

5

Individual Differences Impacting Stressor-Performance Relationships

I n Chapter 4, many studies that have examined the relationship between job-related stressors and a variety of performance indexes were reviewed. As the reader undoubtedly noticed, there was considerable variation among stressor-performance correlations from study to study. Such variation may be due in part to the specific stressor and performance measure examined in each study. It also may be due to what are called *moderator variables*.

The purpose of this chapter is to take an in-depth look at potential moderators of the relationship between stressors and job performance. This will be accomplished by first providing some background on the nature of moderator variables.

This will be followed by an examination of five classes of variables that may function as moderators of the stressor-performance relationship: (a) competence, (b) demographics, (c) personality traits, (d) psychological attachment to work, and (e) social/organizational support.

Moderator Variables

A moderator variable is defined as any variable that affects the relationship between two other variables (Cohen & Cohen, 1983). As an example, suppose that an organization is planning a massive layoff of managerial employees. Further suppose that among these are two of the managers—say Manager Smith and Manager Jones. Manager Smith has a large mortgage on his home and is paying for each of his two children to attend elite private universities. Manager Jones, on the other hand, has no mortgage on his house, no children, and has recently inherited a large sum of money. Which manager do you think will react more negatively to this layoff? Logic would dictate that under the circumstances Manager Smith would react more negatively to this unfortunate turn of events. Another way to describe this somewhat contrived situation would be that "financial and economic resources moderate the impact of being laid off."

Historically, moderator variables have played a very important role in the organizational sciences. That is, most theories of human behavior proposed over the years have made provisions for moderator variables. This is certainly true in the field of occupational stress. In fact, all of the occupational stress models described in Chapter 1 include moderator variables, either explicitly or implicitly. This makes good sense because human behavior is so complex. It is simply unrealistic to assume that all people are impacted by all things in the same manner.

Despite the intuitive appeal of moderator variables, providing evidence for their existence is often problematic. The most common statistical procedure used to detect moderator variables is *moderated multiple regression*. In its simplest form, this involves predicting some outcome variable (e.g., performance) using three other variables. These three variables would include an independent variable (sometimes called the "predictor"), the moderator variable, and a term that represents the interaction between the independent variable and moderator variable (sometimes called the "cross-product term"). A moderated relationship is said to exist when the cross-product term explains a meaningful amount of the variation in the outcome variable.

The problem with moderated multiple regression, in practice, is that it is an extremely *low power* statistical test. A microscope offers a good analogy for understanding statistical power. Specifically, microscopes differ in their sensitivity and hence in their ability to allow the visual identification of different microscopic materials. An electron microscope, for example, allows one to view objects that cannot be detected using a microscope that is less powerful. Due to a variety of factors (i.e., strength of the true relationship between variables, sample size, measurement error), statistical tests also differ in their sensitivity, except, in the case of statistics, the sensitivity is related to the detection of relationships between variables rather than the viewing of microscopic images.

The basic problem with low power tests such as moderated multiple regression is that they often lead researchers erroneously to conclude that no moderator effects exist when, in reality, they actually do. It is important to point out, however, that low statistical power is not a problem that is specific to moderated multiple regression. In fact, this is a general problem in organizational research due, in most cases, to low sample sizes. Mone et al. (1996), for example, estimated that the average level of statistical power in organizational behavior research is around .50 (the possible range is 0 to 1.0). What this means is that, on average, the chance of detecting a true relationship is about 50%. Suffice it to say that organizational researchers are rarely armed with "electron microscopes."

What, the reader may be asking, is the purpose of this brief "statistical digression"? It is simply to alert the reader to the pitfalls associated with the detection of moderator variables as we examine the evidence. The reality is that, in most cases, the "cards are stacked against" finding moderator effects. This suggests that the failure to detect moderator effects must be viewed cautiously. Conversely, when moderator effects are found repeatedly, this may have important substantive implications.

Specific Moderators

Like stressors, there are hundreds, perhaps thousands, of potential moderators of the relationship between job-related stressors and job performance. In order to provide some organization for this portion of the chapter, moderators have been grouped into five different categories: (a) competence, (b) demographics, (c) personality traits, (d) psychological attachment to work, and (e) social/organizational support.

Competence

It seems rather plausible that when faced with a stressor, the performance of employees who are most competent would be affected to a lesser degree than would employees who are less competent. A highly competent employee, one would assume, would be more likely to maintain a high level of performance even in the face of stressors. This relatively straightforward hypothesis, however, begs the question, "What is meant by competence?" Given what we already know about the determinants of job performance (see Chapter 3), an individual can become competent in many ways. For example, competence may be due to innate ability (real or perceived), task experience, or even specific information that facilitates successful coping with stressors. It is important to distinguish between different forms of competence because each may moderate stressor-performance relations for somewhat different reasons.

Although innate ability has not been examined as a moderator in occupational stress research, a strong case can be made for the idea that ability may moderate stressor-performance relations. Payne (1991), for example, makes a very compelling case for ability as a moderator in occupational stress research. Drawing on Sternberg's (1985) triarchic theory of intelligence, Payne provides examples of several ways in which high levels of ability could mitigate the impact of stressors on performance. For example, an employee possessing high verbal ability and social competence (two components of intelligence, according to Sternberg's theory) may be more likely to gather information from others that would facilitate coping with a stressor at work. More effective coping, in turn, would allow such an individual to maintain a high level of performance despite being exposed to stressors. Such individuals may also appraise potential stressors (e.g., deadlines, challenging assignments) as less threatening, and thus their performance would be less affected by them. Empirical research has yet to examine the role of ability in occupational stress; however, this would appear to be a fruitful area for further investigations.

Research has examined the moderating effects of several surrogate measures of ability. Schuler (1975), for example, examined whether job level moderated the performance-related effects of role ambiguity and role conflict. It was hypothesized that role ambiguity would be associated with performance decrements only at higher organizational levels because high-level employees frequently must cope with ambiguous situations. On the other hand, it was hypothesized that role conflict would have an impact only at lower organizational levels because such individuals do not have the power to mediate competing job demands. Data from employees of a manufacturing company did not support the proposed hypotheses.

Two other studies have examined what is termed *sense of competence* as a moderator of the relationship between stressors and performance. Bhagat and Allie (1989) defined sense of competence as "individuals' internal, psychological feelings concerning how competent they seem to be to themselves, but not necessarily how competent they really are" (p. 234). They examined this variable as a moderator of the relation between both organizational and personal stressors and job performance among a sample of teachers. It was expected that those who perceived themselves as competent would be able to cope most successfully with stressors. Ratings of teacher performance were provided by principals.

The results of Bhagat and Allie's (1989) investigation indicated that neither organizational or personal stressors were related to performance. Sense of competence, however, was positively related to performance ratings (.24), indicating that those who perceived themselves as more competent also received more favorable ratings. Moderator tests indicated that sense of competence had no moderating effect on relations between either organizational or personal stressors and performance. This result should be viewed cautiously, however, because the sample size for the moderator tests involving job performance was relatively low ($N = 137$), and thus, statistical power may have been lacking.

Borucki (1987) examined the related, though somewhat different, construct of "interpersonal competence" as a moderator of the performance-related effects of role conflict, role ambiguity, and role overload in a sample of first-line managers in a ship-equipment producing company in Gdansk, Poland. In this study, interpersonal competence was defined as the individual's perceived capacity to establish meaningful interpersonal contacts. Given the interpersonal nature of role ambiguity and role conflict (and to a lesser degree, role overload), it was expected that those with a high level of interpersonal competence would be able to cope with these stressors in a way that did not negatively impact their performance.

Like Bhagat and Allie (1989), Borucki (1987) found that interpersonal competence was positively related to self-rated job performance (.21). Employees who rated themselves as being interpersonally competent also rated their performance more favorably. This study found no evidence that interpersonal competence moderated the performance-related effects of any of the stressors. Sample size, in this case, was also rather small ($N = 107$), and thus statistical power may have been inadequate to detect moderator effects.

Another way in which an employee may acquire the competence needed to buffer the performance-related effects of stressors is through job experience. Quinones, Ford, and Teachout (1995), however, point out that there are many ways to measure job experience and all are not equivalent. Specifically, experience can be measured in terms of amount (number of jobs), time (job tenure), or type (type of organization or job where experience has been acquired). Furthermore, experience can be measured at the organizational, job, or task level. These investigators conducted a meta-analysis of the relation between different measures of experience and performance and found that experience measures that assess *amount* and those at the *task* level were most strongly related to performance.

Schuler (1977) examined whether relevant job experience, education, and organization level would jointly moderate the relationship between role stressors (role ambiguity and role conflict) and performance ratings among employees from two organizations—a large manufacturing firm and a large utility. Based on earlier work (Schuler, 1975), it was expected that high levels of job experience and education would moderate the relationship between role ambiguity and performance *only* at higher organizational levels. The logic behind this hypothesis was the assumption that role ambiguity was most likely to be experienced at high, as opposed to low, organizational levels. Given this assumption, it was further reasoned that when faced with ambiguous job demands, employees with higher levels of job experience and education would have the competence to maintain a high level of performance when faced with this stressor.

On the other hand, it was also predicted that high levels of job experience and education would moderate the relationship between role conflict and performance only at *low* organizational levels. In this case it was expected that role conflict would most likely be experienced at lower organizational levels (Schuler, 1975). Similarly, when faced with such competing role demands, it was expected that higher levels of job experience and education would prevent performance decrements. At middle organizational levels, it was expected that job experience and education would moderate the impact of both stressors.

Overall, Schuler's (1977) data failed to support the proposed hypotheses. However, in one of the two organizations studied (the manufacturing firm), role ambiguity had a more negative impact on job performance among those who lacked relevant job experience. This finding partially supports one of the hypotheses. This moderator effect, however, occurred regardless of organization level and therefore was not what was actually predicted.

More recently, Michaels and Dixon (1994) examined job experience (measured by job tenure) as a moderator of the performance-related effects of role conflict and role ambiguity among a sample of industrial salespersons and a sample of purchasing agents. It was hypothesized, as in the previous studies reviewed, that role stressors would have the most negative impact on the performance of those with the least job tenure. Performance in both samples was measured through self-ratings. Results of this study showed that role ambiguity was negatively related to job performance in the sample of purchasing agents (−.23), whereas role conflict was unrelated. Neither stressor was related to job performance in the industrial sales sample.

Job tenure was unrelated to performance in both samples. Of primary interest, however, was the fact that job tenure had no moderating effects in either sample. This finding may simply be due to the fact that job tenure is not a very meaningful indicator of competence, at least with regard to the performance-related effect of stressors (Quinones et al., 1995). Unfortunately, job tenure is probably the most common measure of experience used in organizational research.

Compared to ability and experience, a much more direct way to facilitate employees' competence in the face of stressors is to provide them with preparatory information before the stressor occurs. There are many types of preparatory information that can be provided. For example, an employee may be provided with *sensory information,* that is, information regarding the feelings that are likely to be experienced when a stressor is encountered. An employee may also be provided *procedural information,* that is, information regarding the nature of the stressful environment. Finally, an employee may be provided with *instrumental information,* that is, information regarding techniques that can be used to counteract the effects of the stressor(s).

Unfortunately, until very recently, most of the literature on preparatory information has come from the medical literature, where it has been shown that such information may mitigate negative emotional reactions to medical procedures (e.g., Johnson & Leventhal, 1974). Recently, however, Inzana, Driskell, Salas, and Johnston (1996) conducted a controlled laboratory investigation in which they assessed whether preparatory information could mitigate the performance-related effects of a stressful task environment.

Participants in this study were a sample of enlisted navy personnel who performed a simulation involving the use of information available on a radar screen to make a series of decisions about the status of an aircraft. This task is similar to that which is performed in a Combat Information Center located on a naval aircraft carrier. Stressors were created during task performance by increasing the task load, providing auditory distractions, and imposing time pressure. All three types of preparatory information (sensory, procedural, and instrumental) were provided to some participants, whereas others received only general instructions.

The major finding from this study was that participants who performed the task while exposed to stressors after receiving preparatory information made fewer errors than those exposed to stressors after receiving only general information. The *speed* with which they performed the task was unaffected by either stressors or preparatory information. This study clearly shows that providing employees with preparatory information prior to their experiencing a stressor may in fact reduce performance decrements. This has direct implications for the design of stress management programs and other organizational interventions that may be used to reduce the impact of stressors.

Despite the considerable value of the Inzana et al. (1996) study, it is somewhat limited in two respects. First, it does not address the issue of whether preparatory information would lessen the impact of stressors that are more chronic in nature, although some related literature suggests that this might be the case. For example, it has been shown that providing job applicants with realistic job previews increases employee retention (Wanous & Colella, 1989). Second, the study examines a fairly limited performance domain (e.g., identification of aircraft). Thus, it is unclear whether preparatory information would be as useful if the performance domain were more complex. Further research is needed to address both of these issues.

Demographics

Although several demographic variables could potentially affect the relationship between stressors and performance, age and gender are the only two that have received more than passing attention in the occupational stress literature. Furthermore, even the attention that has been given to these two demographic characteristics has been more conceptual than empirical.

Age may be an important moderator variable in the occupational stress process for a number of reasons. For example, age may have an impact on the meaning and level of threat associated with a potential stressor. For example, a lack of career progress may be an important stressor to an employee at age 40 but have little impact on an employee nearing retirement. It is also true that certain physical, cognitive, and emotional changes may occur with age. Such changes could adversely affect one's level of performance when faced with stressors. On the other hand, with age comes experience, and such experience may actually buffer the effects of some types of stressors.

Empirical evidence on the impact of age on relations between stressors and performance is sparse. The most consistent finding is that older employees may have trouble adjusting to jobs in which they have little control over the pace at which their tasks are to be completed (Brown, 1957; Chase, 1974). This is due largely to age-related changes in speed of cognitive processing (Sharit & Czaja, 1994). What is unclear, however, is whether the experience that comes with age can offset this effect. Salvendy (1972), for example, found that when performing a machine-paced task, older employees conserved their energy more effectively than younger employees.

This finding implies that, due to their experience, many older employees may possess more effective coping skills than younger employees. Those who do not develop such skills may either self-select out of jobs that contain numerous stressors or may leave involuntarily due to poor performance. Although this hypothesis has not been tested directly, it is consistent with research showing that older employees tend to report fewer psychological and emotional strains than younger employees (Koch, Tung, Gmelch, & Swent, 1982; Motowidlo et al., 1986). Clearly, more research examining age as a moderator of relations between stressors and performance is needed.

Despite increasing numbers of women in the workforce worldwide, occupational stress researchers have only recently begun to examine the impact of gender. According to Jick and Mitz (1985), men and women may react differently to stressors because of innate genetic/biological differences, differences in the characteristics of jobs, or differences in socialization and upbringing. Although little evidence exists to support the genetic/biological explanation for gender differences, there is some evidence that the characteristics of jobs, and hence the stressors encountered, may differ by gender. For example, Turnage and Spielberger (1991) found that females were more likely than males to report experiencing stressors such as meeting deadlines, periods of inactivity, and frequent changes from boring to demanding activities. More recently, Spielberger and Reheiser (1994) found that females were more likely than males to report the following stressors: inadequate salary, personal insults from customers/colleagues, noisy work area, covering for another employee, assignment of increased responsibility, frequent changes from boring/demanding activities, insufficient personal time, and periods of inactivity.

Taken together, the data reported by Spielberger and colleagues suggest either that women hold different types of jobs than men or that they simply perceive their jobs differently. These gender differences show that many of the stressors reported more frequently by women are associated with low-level, low-control jobs. This is important because a lack of control may have a direct, negative impact on performance (Spector, 1986). It also may moderate relations between stressors and performance because a lack of control may either prevent employees from coping effectively with the stressor or lead them to cope in counterproductive ways (Storms & Spector, 1987). Thus, according to this viewpoint, it is not gender per se that is the moderator variable; rather, it is the characteristics of the jobs that are typically held by women that lead to differences in stressor-performance relations by gender.

As stated above, women may be socialized differently than men, and such differences may affect how they cope with stressors (Jick & Mitz, 1985). While there are certainly individual differences, research has shown that compared to men, women are socialized in a manner that encourages both a sense of dependence and a sense of inability to control their environment (Cochrane & Stopes, 1980). Such differences in socialization may lead to gender differences in the perception of stressors, even when jobs are the same. For example, Murphy, Beaton, Cain, and Pike (1994) examined differences in sources of stress among male and female firefighters. As one might expect, females were more likely than males to report "unfair discrimination" as a source of stress. Interestingly, females were also more likely than males to report "concerns over their job skills" as being a source of stress. This could have clear implications for performance when experiencing job-related stressors, although this was not examined in the study. As with age, more research needs to be done examining whether gender has an impact on relations between stressors and job performance.

Personality Traits

Of all the moderator variables included in this chapter, personality has been studied the most extensively by far. This is not surprising, because the graduate training of many occupational stress researchers has been in psychology. It also reflects the fact that, in general, personality is viewed as an important variable in the organizational sciences (e.g., Mount & Barrick, 1995; see Davis-Blake & Pfeffer, 1989, for a dissenting viewpoint).

Although no attempt will be made to provide a comprehensive, all-inclusive definition of *personality,* it is important to provide defining characteristics because this term is often misused. The most common defining characteristic among psychologists is that personality characteristics are viewed as *stable traits.* That is, personality does not change much throughout a person's lifetime; in general, empirical data have supported this (Eysenck, 1989). Because of this, many psychologists assume that personality traits have a *genetic basis*. Unfortunately, this is rather difficult to demonstrate empirically because of the difficulty of designing research that can clearly separate genetic from environmental influences (Cropenzano & James, 1990). A final defining characteristic of personality is that it is only meaningful in the context of observable behavior. That is, one can only know another's personality as it is reflected in the person's behavior, because it is impossible truly to know another person's inner thoughts and feelings. Indeed, we often use personality traits (e.g., introverted, impulsive) to explain, understand, and, in some cases, predict others' behavior.

Although numerous personality traits have been examined in the occupational stress literature (Jex & Beehr, 1991), only three have been examined as moderators of the relation between stressors and job performance. Historically, the personality trait that has received the greatest attention in occupational stress research has been the Type A Behavior Pattern (hereafter, Type A). As the name suggests, the Type A is actually a *combination* of behaviors and personality traits (Friedman & Rosenman, 1974). Personality traits that are typical of Type A individuals include hostility, irritability, competitiveness, and a strong sense of time urgency. Typical Type A behaviors include a high activity level, explosive speech patterns, and visible displays of annoyance and impatience either when interrupted or when slowed down (i.e., stuck in traffic). The term Type B is used to describe those individuals who demonstrate characteristics opposite of those of Type A.

Ever since the introduction of the Type A trait, it has been proposed that this may moderate stressor-strain relations (Ganster, 1987). The major reasoning behind this proposition is that Type A individuals are more physiologically reactive to stressors compared to Type Bs (e.g., Suarez & Williams, 1990). That is, when faced with stressors, Type A individuals may exhibit greater elevation in heart rate and blood pressure compared to Type Bs. It has also been suggested that Type A individuals may self-select into occupations that contain more stressors.

Early Type A research relied primarily on what are termed *global* measures. That is, an individual would complete either a paper-and-pencil test or a structured interview. On the basis of his or her responses, the individual would be classified as either Type A or Type B. In the past 10 years, this approach has been criticized because different components of the Type A trait have been shown to have different effects (e.g., Edwards & Baglioni, 1991). An alternative approach that has gained some popularity among researchers has been to assess the two components,

"Achievement Strivings" (e.g., working hard) and "Impatience-Irritability" (e.g., showing annoyance with others; Barling, Kelloway, & Cheung, 1996; Spence, Helmreich, & Pred, 1987). Researchers have essentially captured the positive aspects of Type A in Achievement Strivings and the negative aspects in Impatience-Irritability.

Over the years, Type A research has focused largely on the health-related consequences of this personality trait (Ganster, 1987). Recently, however, the performance-related effects have begun to be examined. For example, Lee, Ashford, and Bobko (1990) examined whether perceived control interacted with Type A to impact performance. They hypothesized that Type A would be positively related to performance only among employees who perceived that they had a great deal of control at work. Essentially, what these authors are arguing is that Type A individuals would thrive in situations where they perceive they have control over the work environment. Type A individuals were not expected to perform as well when perceived control was low. This study did not examine Type A as a moderator, although it is certainly relevant to the issue. As expected, Type A was strongly related to performance (supervisory ratings) when perceived control was high (.51). In contrast, when perceived control was low, there was no relationship between Type A and performance (.01).

Despite the strength of the findings, one problem with the Lee et al. (1990) study was that Type A was assessed with a global measure (the Thurstone Temperament Schedule's Activity subscale; Thurstone, 1953). Thus, the findings do not reveal which Type A *component* affects employee reactions to perceived control. Research using component measures, however, has shown rather consistently that Achievement Strivings is positively related to performance, while Impatience-Irritability is unrelated (Bluen, Barling, & Burns, 1990; Lee, 1992; Lee, Ashford, & Jamieson, 1993; Spence et al., 1987). It is therefore quite possible that a *lack* of perceived control has more negative performance-related effects among employees who report a high level of the Achievement Strivings dimension. This may be due to the fact that low perceived control may be seen as a barrier to task performance—something that is very important to those high on Achievement Strivings. In contrast, findings that have shown that Type As tend to experience the most physiological and psychological strain when confronted with low-control situations (e.g., Ivancevich & Matteson, 1988) may be reflecting the Impatience-Irritability dimension. Future research needs to examine whether Achievement Strivings and Impatience-Irritability moderate relations between other occupational stressors (e.g., role ambiguity, role conflict, situational constraints) and performance.

Although Achievement Strivings may moderate the effects of perceived control, there is research suggesting that perceptions of control may affect the *expression* of Impatience-Irritability. Benight and Kinicki (1988) conducted a laboratory experiment in which university students performed a task (an in-basket simulation; Cascio, 1991) under either moderately or highly uncontrollable conditions. Through observations, they found that subjects exhibited behavioral manifestations of Type A (e.g., degree of mental and emotional alertness, speed of local motion, body restlessness, facial grimaces, and hand movements) when the task was performed under conditions of *moderate* uncontrollability.

Because the behaviors examined by Benight and Kinicki (1988) seem most strongly associated with Impatience-Irritability, it is possible that this Type A dimension may become more prominent when perceived control is moderately low. Whether the increased expression of Impatience-Irritability leads to performance decrements is unknown, although considerable evidence has shown that Impatience-Irritability is associated with health problems (Barling & Charbonneau, 1992; Lee, 1992; Spence et al., 1987), which could ultimately detract from performance. It is also possible that a high level of Impatience-Irritability could have a negative effect on the performance of some jobs (e.g., those requiring customer contact) more than others (e.g., those requiring solitary effort). Thus, researchers exploring the effects of Type A in the future would be wise to pay attention to the nature of the work being performed.

A second personality characteristic that has been explored as a moderator of the relationship between job stressors and performance is *self-esteem*. Self-esteem is defined as the degree to which a person "expresses an attitude of approval or disapproval, and indicates the extent to which the individual believes self to be capable, significant, successful, and worthy" (Coopersmith, 1967, pp. 4-5). Another way to define self-esteem would simply be the extent to which a person likes him- or herself.

As one might guess, researchers have tested the notion that stressors have greatest negative impact on the performance of employees with low self-esteem. Why might low self-esteem have this effect? One explanation comes from Brockner's (1983, 1988) so-called *plasticity hypothesis,* which states that individuals with low self-esteem are more influenced by events in the social environment (i.e., their behavior is more "plastic") than their high self-esteem counterparts. Because job stressors typically occur in the social environment, low self-esteem tends to increase reactivity to stressors and hence performance. It has also been shown that individuals with low self-esteem possess other characteristics that would increase the likelihood that they would perform lower when faced with stressors. For example, such individuals tend to lack initiative and self-confidence (Brockner, 1988) and to use more passive forms of coping with stressors than those with high self-esteem (Kinicki & Latack, 1990).

Two frequently cited studies examining self-esteem as a moderator of the relationship between stressors and performance were performed by Mossholder, Bedeian, and Armenakis (1981, 1982). In the 1981 study, these researchers examined whether self-esteem moderated relations between role stressors (role ambiguity and role conflict) and performance ratings among a sample of hospital professionals and support staff. The results showed that self-esteem indeed moderated the performance-related impact of role conflict (but not role ambiguity) in a manner that was consistent with Brockner's (1983) plasticity hypothesis. That is, role conflict was negatively related to job performance only among those reporting low self-esteem. It is important to note, however, that this moderator effect occurred only for employees at *low* levels of the organization studied. The authors actually predicted that this would be the case, because employees at lower organizational levels typically have less power to cope with competing role demands than employees at higher levels.

In their 1982 study, Mossholder and colleagues again examined self-esteem as a moderator variable, this time among a sample of nursing employees at a large hospital. The stressor in this study consisted of employee ratings of the quality of peer group interactions within autonomous work groups. Performance was again measured via supervisory ratings. The results showed that self-esteem produced a strong moderator effect. Quality of peer group interactions was strongly related to performance only among those reporting low self-esteem. As expected, performance was lowest among those who perceived peer group interactions to be of low quality. In contrast, quality of peer group interaction was essentially unrelated to performance among those who reported high levels of self-esteem.

Since the work by Mossholder et al. (1981, 1982), relatively little research has examined self-esteem as a moderator of relations between stressors and performance, although several recent studies have focused on physical and psychological outcomes (e.g., Allen, 1993; Ganster & Schaubroeck, 1991b; Jex, Cvetanovski, & Allen, 1994; Jex & Elacqua, in press). One recent study of self-esteem that examined performance was conducted by Pierce, Gardner, Dunham, and Cummings (1993). Earlier, these authors had examined the moderating effects of what they termed *organization-based* self-esteem and provided the following definition: "Organization-based self-esteem reflects the self-perceived value that individuals have of themselves as organizational members acting within an organizational context" (Pierce, Gardner, Cummings, & Dunham, 1989, p. 625). These authors reasoned that using organization-based self-esteem was more appropriate than global self-esteem (which had been used in past studies) because role stressors and performance were measured from an organizational frame of reference. The argument supporting the moderating effects of organization-based self-esteem was the same as that for global self-esteem (e.g., the plasticity hypothesis).

Based on data from a sample of managerial, supervisory, administrative, and engineering employees of an electrical utility company, it was found that organization-based self-esteem moderated the performance-related effects of role ambiguity, (lack of) work environment support, and (lack of) supervisory support. In all three cases, these stressors were negatively associated with performance ratings only among those reporting low levels of organization-based self-esteem, whereas there was essentially no relationship among those reporting high levels. No moderator effects were found for role conflict or role overload. This may have been due to the fact that employees in this study came from the managerial/professional ranks. As was pointed out earlier, it has been argued, at least for role conflict, that self-esteem should have a moderating effect on this stressor only at low organizational levels (Mossholder et al., 1981).

A final personality trait that has received some attention as a moderator in occupational stress research is *locus of control*. According to Rotter (1966), locus of control is a relatively stable personality trait that affects individuals' perceptions of the amount of control they have over reinforcements in their lives. Individuals who possess an *internal* locus of control believe that they are able to exert control over reinforcements. Individuals who possess an *external* locus of control believe that reinforcements are controlled by luck, fate, or possibly other people. Most researchers conceptualize locus of control to be on a continuum from highly external to highly internal.

As might be expected, locus of control is related to a number of important work outcomes. For example, Spector (1982) reviewed the theoretical and empirical literature on the organizational implications of locus of control and concluded that, in general, an internal locus of control should be associated with more desirable employee outcomes (e.g., lower turnover, higher performance, greater job satisfaction) than an external locus of control. Research conducted since Spector's review has generally supported these assertions (e.g., Cvetanovski & Jex, 1994; Fisher, 1995; Spector & O'Connell, 1994).

With regard to occupational stress, locus of control would appear to be relevant in two distinct ways. First, it is likely that employees with an internal locus of control, so-called internals, *desire* more autonomy, control, and participation in decisions than externals and therefore react more favorably when their jobs possess these characteristics (Giles, 1977; Runyon, 1973). Conversely, internals may react more negatively than externals when these things are lacking. Second, because internals believe they have more control over things in their environment, it is likely that they would cope more effectively with stressors than externals. In fact, this has been supported with regard to the relationship between situational constraints and both job satisfaction and motivation (Freedman & Phillips, 1985). Specifically, situational constraints were found to be most strongly related to dissatisfaction and low motivation among externals.

While no study has directly examined locus of control as a moderator of relations between stressors and job performance, there is some evidence that such a moderated relationship may exist. Storms and Spector (1987), for example, found that *work* locus of control (e.g., locus of control specific to work settings) moderated the relationship between self-reports of perceived frustration and sabotage among a sample of employees of a mental health center. As expected, frustration was more strongly related to reports of sabotage among those reporting an external work locus of control. These authors reasoned that employees with an internal work locus of control would be more likely to react to frustration in productive ways (e.g., voicing their concerns). Given that frustration is a strong correlate of many stressors (e.g., Spector, 1997b), locus of control may be a key factor in determining whether or not employees react to stressors by engaging in counterproductive behaviors.

Psychological Attachment to Work

Employees may differ considerably in their level of psychological attachment to work. The term *psychological attachment* is used here to encompass several variables indicating the extent to which persons see their job, career, or employing organization as being important. Indicators of psychological attachment that have been studied in the organizational sciences over the years include job involvement (Lodahl & Kejner, 1965), career commitment (Schein, 1978), professional commitment (Landy & Guion, 1970), and organizational commitment (Mathieu & Zajac, 1990; Mowday, Steers, & Porter, 1979).

Of all these variables, the only ones that have been examined as moderator variables are organizational commitment and professional commitment. Jamal (1984), in a study described in Chapter 3, argued that employees who are highly committed to their employing organization and profession should not react as negatively to stressors as those who are less committed. He argued that employees who are highly committed to their employing organization have a higher level of trust and are more loyal. As a result, they are more likely to cope with stressors in a way that does not adversely affect performance. Employees who are highly committed to their profession, it was argued, will possess greater job knowledge and thus will be less surprised by certain stressful aspects of the job. This greater knowledge will lead to more adaptable responses to stressors.

Based on data from a sample of nurses employed by a large hospital, Jamal's (1984) propositions regarding organizational and professional commitment were partially supported. Organizational commitment had a strong moderating effect on the relationship between role overload and all three indicators of job performance (quality of performance, level of motivation, and level of interest in patient care). In all cases, role overload was most strongly associated with performance decrements among those reporting a low level of organizational commitment. Organizational commitment also moderated the performance-related effects of role ambiguity and role conflict, although to a lesser degree. Professional commitment moderated the effects of role overload in the same manner as organizational commitment but had no impact on any of the other stressors.

Organizational commitment was also examined as a moderator variable in another previously described study conducted by Jamal (1985). In this case, however, the moderator hypothesis was tested in a sample of managerial employees and a sample of blue-collar employees. In addition, measures of performance (quantity of performance, quality of performance, and effort exerted) were somewhat different than those used in the 1984 study of nurses.

In the managerial sample, organizational commitment moderated relations among each of four stressors (role ambiguity, role overload, role conflict, and resource inadequacy), a composite stressor index, and at least one of the performance indicators. In all cases, stressors were more strongly associated with lower levels of performance among those reporting low levels of organizational commitment. The moderator effects found in the blue-collar sample were quite similar to those found in the managerial sample.

One difference worth noting in the findings between the two samples was that organizational commitment had a more consistent moderating effect on the relationship between stressors and level of effort exerted in the blue-collar sample. This may simply reflect differences in the performance domains of these two types of employees. Compared to managerial employees, blue-collar employees may have had relatively less control over quantity or quality of performance. In contrast, these employees probably had more relative control over their level of effort. Thus, when commitment was lacking, reducing effort may have been the most logical (and feasible) way for the blue-collar employees to cope with stressors in the workplace.

Since Jamal's (1984, 1985) work, little occupational stress research has been done examining organizational commitment as a moderator variable. This is unfortunate, because the organizational commitment construct has undergone considerable refinement in the past 10 years. For example, organizational commitment researchers now distinguish among *attitudinal, continuance,* and *normative* forms of commitment (Meyer & Allen, 1997). Attitudinal commitment reflects a genuine identification with one's employing organization and its goals. Continuance commitment, on the other hand, reflects commitment based on one's "sunk costs" within the organization. For example, an employee who has been employed by an organization for several years has likely accumulated vacation time, pension funds, and seniority that would be lost if that person were to leave the organization. Normative commitment reflects a belief on the part of the employee that remaining with the organization is morally right or just. In considering these three forms of commitment, it is important to note that they are not mutually exclusive. In most cases, an employee is committed to his or her employing organization for all three reasons, although the relative emphasis may vary among individuals.

What implication does this distinction in forms of organizational commitment have for studying the moderating effect of organizational commitment on the relationship between stressors and job performance? It seems logical that attitudinal and normative commitment would be most likely to moderate stressor-performance relations in the manner found by Jamal (1984, 1985). One would think that a person who identifies with his or her employing organization and is committed to its goals or who believes that being committed is the right thing to do would find a way to cope with stressors in a way that does not impair job performance. In contrast, when organizational commitment is based primarily on "sunk costs" there is no reason why an employee would maintain a high level of performance in the face of stressors. In fact, in this case the presence of a stressor might be viewed as an excuse for withholding effort and hence reduced levels of performance.

Social/Organizational Support

In this final category of moderator variables, two separate but related variables are grouped together. Generally speaking, *social support* reflects the availability of other people to help employees when they experience workplace stressors (Gore,

1987). Cohen and Wills (1985) state that support from others can be described along two dimensions: structural versus functional and emotional versus tangible. When support is viewed in terms of *structure,* this refers to whether or not an employee is embedded in a social network that could potentially provide support. On the other hand, when support is viewed in terms of *function,* this refers to whether or not a given member of one's social network (e.g., supervisor) actually provides support. The "emotional versus tangible" dimension of social support simply refers to the various ways in which support can be provided. Providing *emotional* support might involve listening to the stressed individual and helping reduce his or her anxiety. *Tangible* support, in contrast, involves the provision of support in a way that may actually alleviate the stressor being experienced. An example of this might be taking on some of the tasks of a coworker who is overloaded.

In general, it has been proposed that the effects of social support can be characterized in one of three ways (Beehr, 1985, 1995; Cohen & Wills, 1985). First, a high level of support from others may result in lower levels of stressors in the work environment. This would appear to be most likely when tangible forms of support are offered (Fenlason & Beehr, 1994). Second, high levels of social support may directly reduce levels of psychological, physical, and behavioral strain. That is, even if stressors still exist, the existence of support may provide some comfort. Finally, it has also been proposed that social support "buffers" the effects of stressors. Stated differently, the relationship between stressors and strains exists only for those who lack social support.

In recent years, considerable occupational stress research has examined the impact of social support (see Gore, 1987, and Beehr, 1995, for summaries of this literature). Overall, the main effect of social support has been demonstrated most consistently by researchers. That is, high levels of social support have been associated with lower levels of psychological strains such as anxiety, depression, and tension. In contrast, support for the buffering effect has been quite mixed. Unfortunately, very little work has examined whether social support impacts the relationship between stressors and performance. Furthermore, the few studies that have examined performance as an outcome (e.g., Beehr, King, & King, 1990; Kaufmann & Beehr, 1986) have shown that social support has neither main nor buffering effects.

Given the evidence, as limited as it is, it is tempting to conclude that social support has no impact on the relationship between stressors and job performance. However, this conclusion may be premature for two primary reasons. First, social support researchers continue to disagree on both the meaning and the measurement of social support. As Beehr (1995) has recently lamented, "Given the looseness of definitions in the literature, it is perhaps as difficult to say what social support is not as to say what it is" (p. 183). Perhaps at this point in time, the construct of social support simply has not been defined or measured in a manner that would impact stressor-performance relations.

A second and somewhat more intriguing possibility is that some "third variable" may determine when social support has an impact on relations between stressors and performance. Gender, education, and job type (e.g., blue- vs. white-collar) have been examined in this regard, but no evidence has shown that any of these variables impact the buffering effect of social support (Dunseath & Beehr, 1991; Ganster, Fusilier, & Mayes, 1986). A study by Orpen (1982), however, suggests that social support may indeed be more important for some employees than others. Orpen found that social support from peers and leaders buffered the relationship between role stressors (role ambiguity and role conflict) and super-visory ratings of performance *only* among black employees of several South African federal agencies, whereas no buffering effect was found for white employees.

Given the racial discrimination that existed in South Africa at the time of this study, Orpen (1982) reasoned that black employees attached more significance to social support than their white counterparts. Most important, this study suggests that the process by which social support impacts the effects of job stressors is quite complex. This may help reconcile the mixed findings regarding buffering effects and suggests that future social support research should be aimed at identifying variables and conditions that impact the value of social support.

Another way in which support can be provided to employees is at a more macro organizational level. According to Eisenberger, Huntington, Hutchinson, and Sowa (1986), *perceived organizational support* reflects the degree to which employees perceive their *employing organization* as being committed to them and providing meaningful psychological support. How is perceived organizational support determined? James and James (1989) proposed that the basic dimension of *organizational climate* is the extent to which employees perceive the climate within the organization to be beneficial versus threatening. It is unlikely that an employee who perceives a threatening organizational climate would perceive a high level of support. Employees may also determine the level of support through other mechanisms, such as organizational policies and interactions with other members of the organization (e.g., peers, immediate supervisor).

Although perceived organizational support has not been examined as a moderator variable in occupational stress research, there is some evidence that it is quite relevant to the topic. For example, Jones et al. (1995) found that perceived organizational support was strongly related to job stressors, job satisfaction, and organizational commitment in three samples (manufacturing employees, Canadian federal public service employees, and special education employees). These researchers also found evidence that support may serve as a *mediator* of the effects of stressors. That is, the first response employees may have when they encounter a stressor is a feeling that the organization is not supportive. This may, in turn, lead to negative consequences.

Future research investigating perceived organizational support as a moderator of the relation between stressors and performance may prove to be quite fruitful. Theoretically, it seems quite plausible that employees who feel supported by their organization would be most likely to cope with stressors in a manner that does not lead to performance decrements. A high level of support may lead to greater commitment on the part of the employee. It may also enhance feelings of competence and self-esteem, both of which may facilitate performance.

Focusing on perceived organizational support as a moderator, compared with other moderators that have been discussed in this chapter, may also prove to be more useful to practicing managers. Specifically, changing the level of support within an organization, although presumably not easy, is undoubtedly more feasible than changing such moderators as personality traits. For example, organizations can train managers to be more supportive to employees through interpersonal skills training and perhaps to put greater emphasis on developing and coaching subordinates.

Conclusion

In this chapter, a number of variables were examined that may moderate the relationship between job stressors and job performance. Specifically, the classes of variables included (a) competence, (b) demographics, (c) personality traits, (d) psychological attachment to work, and (e) social/organizational support. Given the lack of direct empirical evidence examining moderator effects, one obvious conclusion to be drawn from this chapter is that more work needs to be done. Perhaps more important, though, more *theoretically and methodologically sound* moderator investigations are needed. As was discussed at the beginning of this chapter, moderator tests more often than not are plagued by methodological problems that result in low statistical power (Aguinis & Stone-Romero, 1997). Combined with the fact that in many cases moderator tests are conducted with

insufficient theoretical justification, it is not surprising that relatively few moderator effects are found in the organizational sciences.

Of the moderator variables reviewed in this chapter, none stands out as being
more powerful than the rest. In general, however, the evidence suggests that
employees are *least* likely to exhibit performance decrements when faced with
stressors under the following conditions: (a) They understand the nature of the
stressor and what to expect when it occurs (Inzana et al., 1996); (b) they possess a
high level of either global or organization-based self-esteem (Mossholder et al.,
1981, 1982; Pierce et al., 1993); (c) they exhibit a low level of the Type A behavior
pattern (if lack of perceived control is the stressor; Lee et al., 1990); and (d) they
have a high level of commitment to their employing organization (Jamal, 1984,
1985).

What is heartening about these conclusions is that, with the possible exception
of Type A, managers in organizations do have some control over these moderators.
That is, managers can help employees to understand the stressors in their work
environment (e.g., through proper orientation and training), can take steps to help
boost employee self-esteem (e.g., through praise), and can often help foster
organizational commitment (e.g., being flexible when an employee has a family
emergency). To the extent that such actions are taken, employees may be better
able to cope with stressors in a way that does not severely detract from performance.

Other moderator variables discussed in this chapter simply have not been
examined enough for any meaningful conclusions to be drawn. This is particularly
true for "macro" variables such as perceived organizational support, because
moderators examined in occupational stress research have traditionally been
characteristics of the individual employee. In a sense, it is disappointing that more
progress has not been made in identifying and documenting moderator variables.
On a more optimistic note, this lack of progress suggests that several new and
exciting avenues for future research exist.

6

Future Issues in the Study of Occupational Stress and Job Performance

Compared to other areas in the organizational sciences, the study of occupational stress is really in its infancy. Furthermore, our understanding of the impact of job-related stressors on performance clearly lags behind our understanding of psychological and physical outcomes. In this final chapter, three issues are discussed that I believe should receive greater attention in the future if we are going to (a) increase our understanding of the performance-related effects of job-related stressors and (b) use that greater understanding to make organizations more productive and ultimately improve employee quality of life. The chapter concludes with a number of summary points regarding the future investigation of occupational stress and job performance.

Stress and Organizational Performance

The vast majority of occupational stress research and theorizing over the years has been focused at the *individual* level of analysis. That is, researchers and theorists have been interested in whether *individuals* who experience job-related stressors also tend to experience psychological, physical, or behavioral problems as a result. It is important to note, however, that we can just as easily ask the question, "Do *organizations* perform poorly when individual employees, as a group, experience many workplace stressors?"

This is an interesting question that has as yet received relatively little attention in the occupational stress literature. Why is this the case? One reason is the difficulty associated with measuring organizational performance (Pritchard, 1992). Just as with individual performance (e.g., Campbell, 1990), there are numerous ways in which organizational performance can be assessed (e.g., profits, stock value, sales volume, level of service provided to customers, etc.), and it is unclear which is the most appropriate. A second and perhaps more important reason is that there is very little theory to guide such investigations. As a result, the mechanisms by which stressors may affect the performance of organizations as a whole are largely unknown. Some recent group and organizational-level research (e.g., Bliese & Halverson, 1996; Ostroff, 1992) suggests that stressors may lead to a reduction in cooperative behavior or to an increase in general levels of distress within groups or organizations. Such conditions may in turn impair group or organizational performance. Unfortunately, there has been little effort (either empirical or theoretical) among occupational stress researchers to explain the link between stressors and performance at the organizational level of analysis.

Despite the relative lack of attention, some studies have examined the relation between stressors and performance-related variables at the organizational level of analysis. For example, Jones et al. (1988) found a positive relationship between scores on a composite stress measure and number of malpractice claims among a sample of hospitals. Hospitals where employees reported higher levels of "stress" had greater numbers of malpractice claims filed by patients, compared to hospitals where employees reported lower levels. In addition, Moran, Wolff, and Green (1995) reported evidence that organizations in which employees report relatively high levels of stressors also report more instances of employees filing worker's compensation claims compared to organizations in which levels of stressors are lower.

This issue was examined more directly in a recent study by Ryan, Schmit, and Johnson (1996) in which aggregate-level relations between a workload stress index and multiple organizational effectiveness measures (performance, customer service, and employee turnover) were investigated. This study was a clear improvement over previous aggregate-level investigations, due not only to the multiple effectiveness criteria but also to the fact that the data were collected over a 2-year period. Thus, unlike other cross-sectional studies, these investigators could make somewhat stronger inferences with regard to causality.

Based on data collected from 142 branches of a large automotive finance company, workload stress was correlated with five measures of effectiveness when these data were collected at the same point in time. Specifically, *branches* where employees perceived a higher degree of workload stress had (a) lower levels of customer satisfaction, (b) a higher number of delinquent accounts, and (c) a higher rate of employee turnover compared to branches where workload stress was lower. Interestingly, when the organizational effectiveness criteria data were collected a year after the workload stress measure, a somewhat different picture emerged. In this case, a high level of workload stress was associated only with lower levels of customer satisfaction and higher employee turnover.

These findings are both interesting and important to those who wish to understand the relation between work-related stressors and organizational performance. To underscore this point, consider the relation between workload stress and customer satisfaction. This finding suggests that individuals who are experiencing conditions of overwork may fail to provide high-quality service to customers. This makes intuitive sense and suggests a possible mechanism by which stressors experienced by individual employees may ultimately lead to lower levels of organizational performance.

Of course, even if we can show that such a link exists, we are still left with the question, "Why does an employee who is overworked provide poor quality service?" It may be that such an employee is in a bad mood and cannot simply "shift gears" automatically when dealing with a customer. On the other hand, an employee who is overworked simply may not have adequate time to provide high-quality customer service. Obviously, given the findings presented by Ryan et al. (1996), both possibilities could be true.

In order to explore the relationship between occupational stress and organizational performance more effectively, theories are needed that help explain the link between stressors experienced by individual employees and organizational-level outcomes. At this point, such cross-level occupational stress theories simply do not exist, but they are beginning to surface in other areas in the organizational sciences (see Klein, Dansereau, & Hall, 1994, for an excellent discussion of levels of analysis issues). Thus, in the future, occupational stress researchers will have something to guide these theory-building efforts.

As a final note, occupational stress researchers may want to explore relations between stressors and performance at the organizational level for more pragmatic reasons. As has been pointed out in previous chapters, there may simply be too many constraints on individual performance to find a consistent relation between stressors and performance at this level. In contrast, at the organizational level, fewer constraints may exist, and therefore it may be more fruitful to examine this relation at this level. Organizational-level research may also be more useful to managers in their efforts to reduce employee strain. This is because in many cases it is more efficient to intervene at the organizational level (e.g., increasing employee participation) rather than simply teaching individual employees to cope more effectively with stressors (Hurrell, 1995).

Stress and the Changing Workplace

It is certainly true that the workplace has changed dramatically in many ways during the past half century. In fact, it appears that the only constant in our work lives is the fact that things are changing! This section will focus on three changes that I think will have a considerable impact on both the future study of occupational stress and job performance, and organizational efforts to combat the effects of stressors: decreasing use of "jobs," demographic shifts, and skill-based polarization.

Decreasing Use of "Jobs"

For most of us, the "job" is the focus of our working lives. That is, most of us have a concrete set of tasks or duties that essentially define what we do as employees (Levine, 1983). Increasingly, however, organizations are making less and less use of the "job" concept. It is becoming much more common, for example, for employee activities to be driven by participation in project teams and the accomplishment of objectives, rather than by fulfilling the requirements of job descriptions.

According to Bridges (1994), this trend toward "dejobbing" has been driven by two major factors. First, and perhaps most significant, the movement away from jobs allows organizations much greater flexibility in staffing. Not surprisingly, this dejobbing trend is closely linked to the increasing use of temporary or "contingent" employees (see Beard & Edwards, 1995, for an excellent review of the impact of contingent work). Second, many organizations have simply found that using "jobs" as focal points for employee activities is not very effective. Stated differently, employees can "do their jobs" but accomplish very little. Organizations that operate in highly competitive markets cannot remain viable if employees are simply fulfilling the obligations required by their job descriptions.

What impact will dejobbing have on the study of occupational stress in general and, more specifically, the relationship between occupational stress and job performance? At a general level, I believe this trend will have a profound impact. It will essentially force occupational stress researchers to reexamine some fundamental theories and assumptions. As discussed in Chapter 1, the foundation of much occupational stress research over the years has been role theory (Jackson & Schuler, 1985; Kahn et al., 1964; Katz & Kahn, 1978; King & King, 1990). An implicit assumption in role theory is that it is possible, and desirable, for employees to have clearly defined, stable roles. If jobs are eliminated and work is organized around projects and rapidly changing performance objectives, does this assumption remain viable? In this type of work environment, are employee "roles" even relevant?

While the questions posed above are obviously directed at role theory, the potential implications of dejobbing certainly extend to other occupational stress theories. Literally all of the theoretical models discussed in Chapter 1 were developed under the assumption that stressors occur in the context of "jobs." Does this mean that we need to start from "ground zero" and develop entirely new theoretical models of occupational stress? Probably not, because most current occupational stress theories (including those based on role theory) can be modified to account for the trend toward dejobbing. Such modifications, however, will require a critical reexamination of existing theories. In fact, this process could prove to be quite useful, because a critical reexamination of existing theory is long overdue.

Besides the general implications for occupational stress theory, what implication will dejobbing have for our efforts to understand the impact of stressors on performance? Consistent with the point made above, it may lead to a reconsideration of what is considered a stressor in the first place. Perhaps more important, this trend will force a reconsideration of what is meant by "performance." In the vast majority of studies cited throughout this book, performance was measured via supervisory ratings. Supervisory performance rating systems are typically based on how well employees perform behaviors associated with a particular job. What if an employee does not have a job, but rather participates on a number of project teams designed to accomplish various tasks? How, then, do we measure performance? Is individual performance, as has typically been measured, even relevant in such an environment? These questions must be addressed if we are to understand the relationship between workplace stressors and performance in the workplace of the future.

For managers, a work environment without jobs will present some interesting challenges with respect to employee stressors. If employee activity is driven primarily by projects, as opposed to a set of job duties, the risk of stressors such as role overload and role conflict will increase (Joyce, 1986). That is, there may be too many projects and the demands of different projects may be conflicting. Therefore, in a "dejobbed" environment, it will be very important for managers to communicate frequently with subordinates to make sure that workloads are reasonable. It will also be crucial for managers to communicate frequently with their peers, in order to make sure that the demands of various projects do not conflict.

Demographic Shifts

Another trend that has been well documented and will undoubtedly affect the study of occupational stress and performance is shifts in the demographic composition of the workforce. Perhaps the most dramatic of these shifts has been the increase in the age composition of the workforce. Jamieson and O'Mara (1991), for example, report that in 1970 the median age of those in the American workforce was 28. That figure is estimated to increase to nearly *40* by the year 2000! It is estimated that by the year 2020, *one third* of the working population will be 45 years of age or older (Hassell & Perrewe, 1993). Two other notable shifts in the demographic composition of the American workforce include the increased participation of women and a much greater variety of cultures represented in the workplace.

The shift toward an older workforce will have important implications for the study of occupational stress and performance. Perhaps the most important of these is that when it comes to promotional opportunities there will be many more people than "slots." Thus, in the future many employees will be frustrated in their attempts to "move up." This suggests that, for many, a lack of career progression will be a major stressor. If organizations want to retain skilled employees who have not "made it," they will need to develop more creative horizontal career paths. Otherwise, such individuals may leave the organization, or they may remain but perform at a minimally acceptable level. For individual managers, older employees will represent a rich source of wisdom and experience.

Given the increasing numbers of older workers, a logical corollary is that there will be *fewer* younger employees. In fact, it is estimated that by the year 2000, only 16% of the American workforce will be between the ages of 16 and 24 years of age ("Human Capital," 1988). One consequence of this shift is that organizations will find themselves in competition to attract and retain skilled entry-level workers (Jamieson & O'Mara, 1991). This will likely involve compensation but will also extend to other conditions of employment such as promotional opportunities.

Given this competition for younger workers, some employees will be promoted very rapidly and will assume positions of considerable responsibility at a rather young age. As a result, it will become increasingly more common for managers to supervise employees who are older and more experienced than they are. Generally speaking, such an arrangement is not necessarily bad. It does, however, violate the traditional age norms of many cultures (i.e., younger people learn from older people) and could lead to increased levels of some workplace stressors. For example, inexperienced managers may feel overwhelmed by being cast into positions of high pressure and responsibility. These younger managers may also be ill-equipped to provide adequate coaching and performance management to their older colleagues. Conversely, older employees may feel resentful of such arrangements and be reluctant to offer assistance to younger managers. For organizations, this suggests that both formal and informal managerial training efforts will increase in importance.

It was estimated in 1988 that by the year 2000 women would comprise approximately 50% of the American workforce and that six out of seven working-age women would be employed outside the home ("Human Capital," 1988). Based on more recent descriptions of the demographic composition of the U.S. workforce (Berry, 1998; Schultz & Schultz, 1998), both of these predictions have been proven correct. Perhaps most significant is the fact that women are increasingly entering traditionally male-dominated occupations and doing so successfully (Jamieson & O'Mara, 1991).

With respect to occupational stress, the influx of women has clearly led to a much greater awareness of the interface between work and family as a source of stress in organizations. In order to keep this book to a manageable length, the issue of work-family conflict was not examined (the interested reader is referred to Cartwright & Cooper, 1997, for an examination of this issue). In the future, it will become increasingly difficult to study occupational stress without addressing the issue of work-family balance. In considering the impact of workplace stressors on job performance, in particular, it will become necessary to consider the interface between the work lives and family lives of employees. We simply cannot continue to act as if the two occur in isolation from each other.

On a more practical level, the future will likely find more organizations providing on-site child care, flexible work schedules (part-time, job sharing, etc.), and other so-called family-friendly benefits in order to attract and retain qualified women. It is important to note here that family-friendly benefits are not exclusively aimed at or utilized by women. On balance, though, women probably consider such benefits more important than men when making employment decisions. Consider, for example, the favorable publicity associated with being on the list of the most family-friendly companies published by *Working Mother* magazine, a periodical read almost exclusively by women. Readers of this magazine will also note the extensive coverage given to work-family issues.

Despite the importance of family-friendly benefits, I believe that individual managers really hold the key to helping employees (male or female) balance work and family domains. This is because, in many cases, individual managers are given considerable discretion on how benefits such as flexible work hours are utilized. Also, managers communicate to employees whether or not family concerns are seen as an intrusion. Managers therefore need to learn flexibility and tolerance when the work and family demands of employees do conflict.

A second and more general implication of more women in the workforce is that the employment experiences of men and women may become more similar over time. In the previous chapter, it was pointed out that there may be some gender differences in the type of stressors experienced on the job (e.g., Jick & Mitz, 1985; Spielberger & Reheiser, 1994). This may be due, in some cases, to the fact that women are underrepresented in many occupations and may have different experiences as a result. As numbers continue to grow, the gender of a particular job incumbent may become less and less relevant. As a result, there may be greater equality in employment conditions (both good and bad), and therefore less variation in stressors is experienced. This argument would obviously not apply to a stressor such as sexual harassment, when the gender of the person experiencing it is relevant regardless of numerical representation.

The term *cultural diversity* has, in recent years, been the source of much debate and disagreement, much of it quite heated (e.g., Coughlin, 1995), Unfortunately, what's largely been lost in all of this is the *reality* that the U.S. workforce represents a greater mix of ethnicities and cultures than it ever has (Goldstein, 1993). Furthermore, it has been estimated that by the year 2000, 43% of all new entrants into the U.S. workforce will be U.S.-born people of color and immigrants ("Human Capital," 1988). I might add that this trend is occurring not only in the United States but also in Canada (Crawford, 1993) and within the European Community (Rubin, 1991).

Perhaps the most tangible implication of this demographic shift is that many of these new workforce entrants will lack basic skills (e.g., language proficiency, reading skills, etc.) that have largely been taken for granted (Goldstein, 1993). In many cases, this will place organizations of the future in a position of being "schools of last resort," if these individuals are to acquire the skills necessary to perform their jobs. It will also require organizations to become more sensitive to culturally based differences in things such as dress, religious beliefs, and even values.

With respect to occupational stress, greater cultural diversity may have important implications. For example, communication problems may become more prevalent due to differences in language and values. This is important because many workplace stressors are rooted in poor communication processes (e.g., King & King, 1990; Schaubroeck et al., 1993). This may also create more situations that lead to situational constraints and thus more frustration.

Diversity may also, in some cases, force organizations to rethink their efforts to reduce stress in the workplace. As an example, many organizations have adopted participative management practices as a way of increasing employee control and thus reducing stress (e.g., Spector, 1986). Unfortunately, employees from certain cultural backgrounds may not desire more control, and thus such efforts may inadvertently *increase* stress for these individuals. Managers must therefore try to be cognizant of cultural differences that may impact organizational stress management efforts.

Despite the potential negatives, cultural diversity also has the potential to enrich organizations greatly. Differing values and viewpoints may, in the long run, lead to more creative decisions and ultimately to greater levels of organizational effectiveness (Cox, Lobel, & McLeod, 1991). If this is to happen, organizations need to be proactive in their efforts to manage such a multicultural workforce (Jamieson & O'Mara, 1991). This may include multicultural training for managers and possibly the redesigning of some jobs so they do not require a high degree of English language proficiency.

Skill-Based Polarization

The present workforce is, without a doubt, more educated and skilled than at any time in our history. For example, over the past 30 years, the number of workers who have completed a high school education has increased dramatically (Lawler,

1986). Ironically, at the same time there are more and more people entering the workforce who, by all standards, could be considered "functionally illiterate." Consider the following quote describing the average 17-year-old high school student: "Most 17-year-olds in school cannot summarize a newspaper article, write a good letter requesting a job, solve real-life math problems, or follow a bus schedule" ("Human Capital," 1988, p. 129). This statement may strike some as a bit too general, but it nevertheless reflects the reality that more and more young people are entering the workforce without many basic skills that were once taken for granted.

Given the two trends described above, an interesting phenomenon will likely develop in the future with respect to skill levels. Specifically, in many organizations the workforce will be polarized into two groups: those who are both highly educated and possess relevant skills and those who have low levels of education and are lacking in basic skills. For lack of a better term, I have labeled this phenomenon *skill-based polarization.*

Skill-based polarization will have important organizational implications, some of which will be relevant to the study of occupational stress. One is that organizations will be forced to provide much of the basic skills training that was previously provided by the public and private educational system. In fact, workplace training programs aimed at teaching basic reading and math skills are already becoming increasingly prevalent (Goldstein, 1993). It is important to point out, though, that much of this training will fall on the shoulders of individual managers. Organizations will also be forced to redesign many jobs (i.e., reduce the skill requirements) in order to accommodate a workforce lacking in basic skills. This will unfortunately lead to many jobs that are unappealing to those with higher education and skill levels.

Having a large contingent of unskilled, uneducated employees may also exacerbate many of the organizational stressors that were discussed in Chapter 4. For example, employees who have difficulty following verbal or written instructions may make it difficult for others to carry out their job duties and thus may be seen as a type of situational constraint (Peters & O'Connor, 1980). This may also lead to problems in the distribution of workload in certain instances because other employees may have to cover for their unskilled coworkers. It is also possible that unskilled employees may experience "qualitative work overload" in some cases, because they are motivated to perform their job but may lack the skills to do so. Organizations, therefore, may need to alter performance standards and train supervisors to engage in more on-the-job training and coaching activities.

As a final comment, what makes the skill-based polarization phenomenon so ironic is that, given demographic trends (see the previous section), organizations of the future will *need* this contingent of relatively unskilled young people to staff entry-level positions. Thus, whereas organizations in the past would simply select entry-level employees who possessed certain basic skills, organizations in the future (for better or worse) will not have this luxury.

Occupational Stress and the Legal Environment

Of all the topics addressed in this book, the legal implications of occupational stress may be the most complex. This complexity stems from the fact that when we enter the legal realm, much of the research that has formed the cornerstone of this book essentially goes "out the window." To illustrate this point, Marcus (1991) aptly points out, "From a litigation perspective, job stress is whatever the courts or legislators decide it is. Stress has less to do with a job than the law's criteria" (p. 250). Adding to this complexity is the fact that even within the United States, the legal status of job-related stress differs from state to state (Ivancevich, Matteson, & Richards, 1985). Outside of the United States, the legal status of job-related stress is even more complex due to the variety of laws and multinational occupational welfare policies (de Gier, 1995). Thus, a comprehensive discussion of the legal implications is well beyond the scope of this book. Rather, in this section a brief overview will be provided, with a discussion of the implications for the study of occupational stress and job performance.

Without a doubt, the most highly publicized legal implication of job-related stress has been the increase in stress-related worker's compensation claims (Aldred, 1994; Ivancevich et al., 1985; Moran et al., 1995; Mulcahy, 1991). This publicity is justified because, since 1980, the frequency of stress-related worker's compensation claims has increased more than any other type of claim (National Council on Compensation Insurance, 1991). Furthermore, at least in the United States, this increase has created what might be described as a "cottage industry" for attorneys and mental health professionals eager to diagnose and treat compensable stress-related problems (Marcus, 1988).

Job-related stressors could potentially play a role in a worker's compensation case in one of three ways (O'Donnell & Krumreich, 1989). A *physical-mental* claim is one in which a mental disability occurs as a result of a physical injury or trauma. As an example of this, an employee who sustains a back injury may become severely depressed. A *mental-physical* claim is one in which a physical disability or illness occurs as a result of a sudden or gradual emotional stimulus (i.e., stressor) in the workplace. A common example of this category would be an employee sustaining a heart attack following a period of overwork. Finally, a *mental-mental* claim is one in which a mental disability occurs as a result of a sudden or gradual emotional stimulus (i.e., stressor) in the workplace. In this case, an employee may become severely depressed after being reprimanded by his or her immediate supervisor.

Of the three types of claims, the physical-mental has the least significance for the study of occupational stress because there is, in effect, no "stressor" involved in this type of claim. Furthermore, all 50 states in the United States have recognized the legitimacy of this type of claim (Sheridan, 1987). In contrast, in the mental-physical and mental-mental categories, the issue of occupational stress is quite relevant. In each of these types of claims, a gradual or sudden emotional stimulus in the workplace leads to the mental or physical injury. This inevitably introduces more subjectivity into these types of claims compared to the physical-mental variety. As a result, some states fully accept the legitimacy of these claims, whereas others reject them out of hand (Sheridan, 1987).

In many states, however, worker's compensation laws are fairly general, and the legitimacy of stress-related claims is shaped over time by rulings in individual cases (e.g., case law). In Wisconsin, for example, an appellate court recently issued a ruling denying benefits to a custodial employee who experienced chest pains after her work performance was criticized by her supervisor ("Court Denies," 1996). The court ruled that for such a physical condition to be compensable, the stressor would have had to come about as a result of "an unusual event different than the problems they (employees) ordinarily deal with" (p. A3). This decision is consistent with the laws in many states, in that compensation for stress-related conditions (mental or physical) is most likely when the stressor is unusual or out of the ordinary (e.g., observing a coworker's death; National Council on Compensation Insurance, 1988).

Given the subjectivity of work-related mental stress claims, this is obviously an area of concern to organizations. Some writers, in fact, have described the increase in stress-related worker's compensation claims as nothing short of a crisis (e.g., King & Pave, 1985; Marcus, 1988; Shalowitz, 1991). In reality, although potentially very costly, stress-related claims still represent a rather small percentage of the total number of worker's compensation claims filed in the United States and other industrialized nations. Furthermore, based on large-scale occupational stress surveys like the one conducted by Northwestern National Life Insurance Company

(Mulcahy, 1991), one might even conclude that the number of stress-related claims is amazingly *low*. For example, in this survey, 69% of the respondents reported experiencing stress-related illnesses often. Clearly, only a small percentage of those who experience stress-related illnesses ever file worker's compensation claims.

The real importance of stress-related claims, in my opinion, is that they raise the important question: Who is responsible for stress in the workplace? In most countries, laws exist that address health and safety issues in the workplace (Biersner, 1995; de Gier, 1995), and these have clearly placed the responsibility on employers for providing a safe and healthy work environment. These laws typically refer only to physical stressors in the work environment (e.g., noise levels, toxic substances, work hours), and it would be difficult to extend them to many of the stressors that have been covered in this book. Thus, it is unlikely that the issue of occupational stress can be dealt with effectively through existing occupational health and safety legislation.

Who, then, is responsible for nonphysical stressors in the workplace? In many states, court decisions have made it quite evident that such responsibility rests with the employer (King & Pave, 1985; Sheridan, 1987). In contrast, others have argued that the responsibility rests more with the employee (e.g., Meeks, 1984). Like most issues, the truth is probably somewhere in the middle.

Most of the stressors discussed in the book (e.g., role ambiguity, role conflict, interpersonal conflict, situational constraints) are caused, or at least exacerbated, by poor management practices and ineffective organizational policies. This being the case, organizations can do much to keep many stressors at manageable levels by proper selection and training of managers, proper design of jobs, and periodic reviews of organizational policies.

Of course, individual employees also bear some responsibility for workplace stress. This may involve something as general as selecting an occupation that is a good fit with one's skills and personality or perhaps learning more effective ways of coping with situations that cannot be controlled. In the extreme, it may even mean leaving a stressful job or occupation. Placing the responsibility for workplace stress entirely on employers or on individual employees really misses the complexity of this problem.

How is the issue of occupational stress and job performance related to legal liability? Simply stated, a greater understanding of the relationship between stressors and job performance will, in the long run, do much to reduce the frequency of stress-related litigation (Ivancevich et al., 1985; Kottage, 1992; O'Donnell & Krumreich, 1989). Because job performance is often the most visible and salient employee behavior, a sudden drop in performance may alert a manager that job-related stressors are getting to a level that an employee is unable to handle. At that point, an organization could intervene before such an employee is simply unable to cope and files a worker's compensation claim. The scenario described above assumes, of course, that an organization has an effective performance management system. Unfortunately, in many organizations, evaluation and management of performance are such low priorities that managers would have no way of knowing if a performance problem existed.

Concluding Comments

My goal in writing this book was to provide a comprehensive, research-based examination of the relationship between occupational stress and job performance. I have tried to do so in a way that is understandable to those who do not have an extensive background in the behavioral sciences. Also, whenever possible, an effort was made to describe the practical implications of theories and research findings.

I hope that one of the major points readers will take away from this book is that the key to understanding the relationship between workplace stressors and job performance is simply a *greater understanding of job performance*. Much of the inconsistency in studies relating job stressors and job performance is due to the fact that researchers have given little attention to which aspects of job performance should be most impacted by stressors. A greater understanding of job performance will facilitate the development of more informed hypotheses about relations between specific stressors and specific performance dimensions (Fried & Tiegs, 1995). This greater understanding is also very important for managers. If managers really understand what facilitates or inhibits performance, they are in a much better position to diagnose and rectify performance problems that are caused by job-related stressors.

A second general point is that much more research needs to be done on variables that moderate relations between stressors and job performance. A point worth adding here is that future moderator investigations must be methodologically sound and have enough statistical power to detect moderator effects (Aguinis & Stone-Romero, 1997). Specific moderators that appear worthy of future investigation include (but are certainly not limited to) ability, experience, self-esteem, organizational commitment, and organizational support. Moderators are also important for managers, because they may be able to impact things such as employee self-esteem, commitment, and support.

As a final point, the relation between occupational stress and job performance needs to be considered in light of the issues discussed in this final chapter: specifically, considering levels of analysis other than the individual, being aware of changes in the nature of work and the demographics of the workforce, and recognizing the legal ramifications of occupational stress. These, of course, are issues for all occupational stress research, regardless of the outcome examined. They are also critical to organizations and individual managers for guiding efforts to reduce stressors and enhance employee quality of life.

In conclusion, my hope is that this book will generate important new ideas and insights among occupational stress researchers regarding the relationship between occupational stress and job performance. Ideally, such ideas and insights will lead to further research. It is also my hope that this book will prove to be useful and informative to managers and organizational policymakers, because these individuals ultimately hold the key to creating work environments where stressors are kept to manageable levels.

References

Abramis, D. J. (1994). Work role ambiguity, job satisfaction, and job performance: Meta-analysis and review. *Psychological Reports, 75,* 1411-1433.

Ackerman, P. L. (1989). Within-task correlations of skilled performance: Implications for predicting individual differences? (A comment on Henry and Hulin, 1987). *Journal of Applied Psychology, 74,* 360-364.

Adelmann, P. K. (1987). Occupational complexity, control, and personal income: Their relation to psychological well-being in men and women. *Journal of Applied Psychology, 75,* 529-527.

Aguinis, H., & Stone-Romero, E. F. (1997). Methodological artifacts in moderated multiple regression and their effects on statistical power. *Journal of Applied Psychology, 82,* 192-206.

Albanese, R., & Van Fleet, D. D. (1985). Rational behavior in groups: The free riding tendency. *Academy of Management Review, 10,* 244-255.

Aldred, C. (1994, December 5). U.K. ruling focuses attention to job stress. *Business Insurance,* pp. 55-56.

Allen, S. J. (1993). *The moderating effects of self-esteem: A closer look at the relationship between work stress and health.* Unpublished master's thesis, Central Michigan University.

Allen, S. J., & Jex, S. M. (1995, September). *The interaction between chronic stressors and traumatic job events.* Paper presented at the APA/NIOSH Conference "Work, Stress, and Health '95: Creating Healthier Workplaces," Washington, DC.

Alluto, A., & Belasco, J. (1972). A typology for participation in organizational decision-making. *Administrative Science Quarterly, 80,* 286-303.

Ashford, S. J., Lee, C., & Bobko, P. (1989). Content, causes, and consequences of job insecurity: A theory-based measure and substantive test. *Academy of Management Journal, 32,* 803-829.

Austin, J. T., Humphreys, L. G., & Hulin, C. L. (1989). Another view of dynamic criteria: A critical reanalysis of Barrett, Caldwell, and Alexander. *Personnel Psychology, 42,* 583-596.

Averill, J. E. (1973). Personal control over aversive stimuli and its relationship to stress. *Psychological Bulletin, 80,* 286-303.

Bandura, A. (1997). *Self-efficacy: The exercise of control.* New York: Freeman.

107

Barling, J. (1987). Psychological functioning following an acute disaster. *Journal of Applied Psychology, 72,* 683-690.

Barling, J., & Charbonneau, D. (1992). Disentangling the relationship between achievement strivings and impatience-irritability: Dimensions of Type A behavior, performance, and health. *Journal of Organizational Behavior, 13,* 369-377.

Barling, J., Kelloway, E. K., & Cheung, D. (1996). Time management and achievement striving interact to predict car sales performance. *Journal of Applied Psychology, 81,* 821-826.

Barnes, V., Potter, E. H., & Fiedler, F. E. (1983). Effects of interpersonal stress on the prediction of academic performance. *Journal of Applied Psychology, 68,* 686-697.

Barrett, G. V., Caldwell, M., & Alexander, R. (1985). The concept of dynamic criteria: A critical reanalysis. *Personnel Psychology, 38,* 41-56.

Beard, K. M., & Edwards, J. R. (1995). Employees at risk: Contingent work and the psychological experience of contingent work. In C. L. Cooper & D. M. Rousseau (Eds.), *Trends in organizational behavior* (Vol. 2, pp. 109-126). Chichester, UK: Wiley.

Beatty, J., Adhern, S., & Katz, R. (1977). Sleep deprivation and the vigilance of anesthesiologists during simulated surgery. In R. Mackie (Ed.), *Vigilance theory, operational performance and physiological correlates* (pp. 1-18). New York: Plenum.

Beehr, T. A. (1976). Perceived situational moderators of the relationship between subjective role ambiguity and role strain. *Journal of Applied Psychology, 61,* 35-40.

Beehr, T. A. (1985). The role of social support in coping with organizational stress. In T. A. Beehr & R. S. Bhagat (Eds.), *Human stress and cognition in organizations* (pp. 375-398). New York: John Wiley.

Beehr, T. A. (1995). *Psychological stress in the workplace.* London: Routledge & Kegan Paul.

Beehr, T. A., & Bhagat, R. S. (1985). Introduction to human stress and cognition in organizations. In T. A. Beehr & R. S. Bhagat (Eds.), *Human stress and cognition in organizations* (pp. 3-19). New York: John Wiley.

Beehr, T. A., Jex, S. M., Stacy, B. A., & Murray, M. A. (1997). *Work stress and co-worker support as predictors of individual strains and performance.* Manuscript submitted for publication.

Beehr, T. A., King, L. A., & King, D. W. (1990). Social support and occupational stress: Talking to supervisors. *Journal of Vocational Behavior, 36,* 61-81.

Beehr, T. A., & Newman, J. E. (1978). Job stress, employee health, and organizational effectiveness: A facet analysis, model, and literature review. *Personnel Psychology, 31,* 665-699.

Benight, C. C., & Kinicki, A. J. (1988). Interaction of Type A behavior and perceived controllability of stressors on stress outcomes. *Journal of Vocational Behavior, 33,* 50-62.

Bernardin, H. J. (1987). Development and validation of a forced choice scale to measure job-related discomfort among customer service representatives. *Academy of Management Journal, 30,* 162-173.

Berry, L. M. (1998). *Psychology at work: An introduction to industrial and organizational psychology* (2nd ed.). Boston: McGraw-Hill.

Bhagat, R. S., & Allie, S. M. (1989). Organizational stress, personal life stress, and symptoms of life strain: An examination of the moderating role of sense of competence. *Journal of Vocational Behavior, 35,* 231-253.

Bhagat, R. S., McQuaid, S. J., Lindholm, H., & Segovis, J. (1985). Total life stress: A multimethod validation of the construct and its effects on organizationally valued outcomes and withdrawal behaviors. *Journal of Applied Psychology, 70,* 202-214.

Bialek, H., Zapf, D., & McGuire, W. (1977, June). *Personnel turbulence and time utilization in an infantry division* (Hum RRO FR-WD-CA 77-11). Alexandria, VA: Human Resources Research Organization.

Biersner, R. J. (1995). Developing an occupational stress standard: Rule making pitfalls. In L. R. Murphy, J. J. Hurrell, Jr., & G. P. Keita (Eds.), *Job stress interventions* (pp. 389-403). Washington, DC: American Psychological Association.

Bliese, P. D., & Halverson, R. R. (1996). Individual and nomothetic models of job stress: An examination of work hours, cohesion, and well-being. *Journal of Applied Social Psychology, 26,* 1171-1189.

Blix, A. G., Cruise, R. J., Mitchell, B. M., & Blix, G. G. (1994). Occupational stress among university teachers. *Educational Research, 36,* 157-169.

Bluen, S. D., Barling, J., & Burns, W. (1990). Predicting sales performance, job satisfaction, and depression by using the achievement striving and impatience-irritability dimensions of Type A behavior. *Journal of Applied Psychology, 75,* 212-216.

Bonnet, M. H. (1986). Performance and sleepiness following moderate sleep disruption and slow wave sleep deprivation. *Physiology and Behaviour, 37,* 915-918.

Borg, M. G., Riding, R. J., & Falzon, J. M. (1991). Stress in teaching: A study of occupational stress and its determinants, job satisfaction, and career commitment among primary schoolteachers. *Educational Psychology, 11,* 59-75.

Borucki, Z. (1987). Perceived organizational stress, emotions, and negative consequences of stress: Global self-esteem and sense of interpersonal competence as moderator variables. *Polish Psychological Bulletin, 18,* 139-148.

Breaugh, J. A., & Colihan, J. P. (1994). Measuring facets of job ambiguity: Construct validity evidence. *Journal of Applied Psychology, 79,* 191-202.

Bridges, W. (1994). *JobShift: How to prosper in a workplace without jobs.* Reading, MA: Addison-Wesley.

Broadbent, D. E. (1971). *Decision and stress.* New York: Academic Press.

Brockner, J. (1983). Low self-esteem and behavioral plasticity: Some implications. In L. Wheeler & P. R. Shaver (Eds.), *Review of personality and social psychology* (Vol. 4, pp. 237-271). Beverly Hills, CA: Sage.

Brockner, J. (1988). *Self-esteem at work.* Lexington, MA: D. C. Heath.

Brown, R. A. (1957). Age and "paced" work. *Occupational Psychology, 31,* 11-20.

Butterfield, P. S. (1988). The stress of residency. *Archives of Internal Medicine, 148,* 1428-1435.

Campbell, J. P. (1990). Modeling the performance prediction problem in industrial and organizational psychology. In M. D. Dunnette & L. M. Hough (Eds.), *Handbook of industrial and organizational psychology* (2nd ed., Vol. 1, pp. 687-732). Palo Alto, CA: Consulting Psychologists Press.

Campbell, J. P. (1994). Alternative models of job performance and their implications for selection and classification. In M. G. Rumsey, C. B. Walker, & J. H. Harris (Eds.), *Personnel selection and classification* (pp. 33-51). Hillsdale, NJ: Lawrence Erlbaum.

Campbell, J. P., Dunnette, M. D., Lawler, E. E., & Weick, K. E. (1970). *Managerial behavior, performance, and effectiveness.* New York: McGraw-Hill.

Campion, M. A., & Thayer, P. W. (1985). Development and field evaluation of an interdisciplinary measure of job design. *Journal of Applied Psychology, 70,* 29-43.

Cannon, W. B. (1914). The interrelations of emotions as suggested by recent physiological researchers. *American Journal of Psychology, 25,* 256-282.

Caplan, R. D., Cobb, S., French, J. R. P., Jr., Harrison, R. V., & Pinneau, S. R. (1975). *Job demands and worker health: Main effects and occupational differences.* Washington, DC: Government Printing Office.

Caplan, R. D., & Jones, K. W. (1975). Effects of workload, role ambiguity, and Type A personality on anxiety, depression, and heart rate. *Journal of Applied Psychology, 60,* 713-719.

Cartwright, S., & Cooper, C. L. (1997). *Managing workplace stress.* Thousand Oaks, CA: Sage.

Cascio, W. F. (1991). *Applied psychology in personnel management* (4th ed.). Englewood Cliffs, NJ: Prentice Hall.

Chase, R. B. (1974). Survey of paced assembly lines. *Industrial Engineering, 6,* 14-18.

Chen, P. Y., & Spector, P. E. (1992). Relationships of work stressors with aggression, withdrawal, theft and substance abuse: An exploratory study. *Journal of Occupational and Organizational Psychology, 65,* 177-184.

Cochrane, R., & Stopes, R. M. (1980). Factors affecting the distribution of psychological symptoms in urban areas of England. *Acta Psychiatrica Scandinavia, 61,* 445-460.

Cohen, J., & Cohen, P. (1983). *Applied multiple regression/correlation for the behavioral sciences.* Hillsdale, NJ: Lawrence Erlbaum.

Cohen, S., & Wills, T. A. (1985). Stress, social support, and the buffering hypothesis. *Psychological Bulletin, 98,* 310-357.

Cooper, C. L., & Marshall, J. (1976). Occupational sources of stress: A review of the literature relating to coronary heart disease and mental ill health. *Journal of Occupational Psychology, 49,* 11-28.

Coopersmith, S. (1967). *The antecedents of self-esteem.* San Francisco: Freeman.

Cotton, J. L. (1995). Participation's effect of performance and satisfaction: A reconsideration of Wagner. *Academy of Management Review, 20,* 276-278.

Coughlin, E. (1995, November 14). The great divide: Public views, private thoughts. *The Chronicle of Higher Education,* pp. A6-A7.

Court denies benefits for normal job stress. (1996, September 14). *Oshkosh Northwestern,* p. A3.

Cox, T. H., Lobel, S. A., & McLeod, P. L. (1991). Effects of ethnic group cultural differences on cooperative and competitive behavior on a group task. *Academy of Management Journal, 34,* 827-847.

Crawford, M. (1993, May). The new office etiquette. *Canadian Business,* pp. 22-31.

Cronbach, L. J., & Furby, L. (1970). How should we measure "change"—or should we? *Psychological Bulletin, 74,* 68-80.

Cropenzano, R., & James, K. (1990). Some methodological considerations for the behavioral genetic analysis of work attitudes. *Journal of Applied Psychology, 75,* 433-439.

Cvetanovski, J., & Jex, S. M. (1994). Locus of control of unemployed people and its relationship to psychological and physical well-being. *Work & Stress, 8,* 60-67.

Dansereau, F., Jr., Graen, G., & Hagan, W. J. (1975). A vertical dyad linkage approach to leadership within formal organizations: A longitudinal approach to the role making process. *Organizational Behavior and Human Performance, 13,* 46-78.

Davis-Blake, A., & Pfeffer, J. (1989). Just a mirage: The search for dispositional effects in organizational research. *Academy of Management Review, 14,* 385-400.

Deadrick, D. L., & Madigan, R. (1990). Dynamic criteria revisited: A longitudinal study of performance stability and predictive validity. *Personnel Psychology, 43,* 717-744.

de Gier, E. (1995). Occupational welfare in the European community: Past, present, and future. In L. R. Murphy, J. J. Hurrell, Jr., & G. P. Keita (Eds.), *Job stress interventions* (pp. 405-416). Washington, DC: American Psychological Association.

Dunseath, J. L., & Beehr, T. A. (1991, May). *The job stress-social support buffering hypothesis, employee gender, and collar color.* Paper presented at the annual meeting of the Midwestern Psychological Association, Chicago.

Easterbrook, J. A. (1959). The effect of emotion on cue utilization and the organization of behavior. *Psychological Review, 66,* 183-201.

Edwards, J. R. (1994). The study of congruence in organizational behavior research: Critique and a proposed alternative. *Organizational Behavior and Human Decision Processes, 58,* 51-100.

Edwards, J. R., & Baglioni, A. J., Jr. (1991). Relationship between Type A behavior pattern and mental and physical symptoms: A comparison of global and component measures. *Journal of Applied Psychology, 76,* 276-290.

Eisenberger, R., Huntington, R., Hutchinson, S., & Sowa, D. (1986). Perceived organizational support. *Journal of Applied Psychology, 71,* 500-507.

Elliott, R. H., & Jarrett, D. T. (1994). Violence in the workplace: The role of human resource management. *Public Personnel Management, 23,* 287-299.

Eysenck, M. W. (1989). Personality, stress arousal, and cognitive processes in stress transactions. In R. W. J. Neufeld (Ed.), *Advances in the investigation of psychological stress* (pp. 133-160). New York: John Wiley.

Fenlason, K. J., & Beehr, T. A. (1994). Social support and occupational stress: Effects of talking to others. *Journal of Organizational Behavior, 15,* 157-175.

Fisher, T. G. (1995). *Self-efficacy and locus of control: Proposed moderators of the effects of participative decision making.* Unpublished master's thesis, Central Michigan University.

Forsyth, D. R. (1990). *Group dynamics* (2nd ed.). Pacific Grove, CA: Brooks/Cole.

Frankenhaeuser, M. (1979). Psychoneuroendocrine approaches to the study of emotion as related to stress and coping. In H. E. Howe & R. A. Diensbier (Eds.), *Nebraska Symposium on Motivation,* pp. 123-161.

Freedman, S. M., & Phillips, J. S. (1985). The effects of situational performance constraints on intrinsic motivation and satisfaction: The role of perceived competence and self-determination. *Organizational Behavior and Human Decision Processes, 35,* 397-416.

French, J. R. P., Jr., & Kahn, R. L. (1962). A programmatic approach to studying the industrial environment and mental health. *Journal of Social Issues, 18,* 1-47.

Fried, Y., & Ferris, G. R. (1987). The validity of the job characteristics model: A review and meta-analysis. *Personnel Psychology, 40,* 287-322.

Fried, Y., & Tiegs, R. B. (1995). Supervisors' role conflict and role ambiguity differential relations with performance ratings of subordinates and the moderating effect of screening ability. *Journal of Applied Psychology, 80,* 282-291.

Friedland, N., Keinan, G., & Regev, Y. (1992). Controlling the uncontrollable: Effects of stress on illusory perceptions of controllability. *Journal of Personality and Social Psychology, 63,* 923-931.

Friedman, M., & Rosenman, R. H. (1974). *Type A behavior and your heart.* New York: Knopf.

Friedman, R. C., Bigger, J. T., & Kornfield, D. S. (1971). The intern and sleep loss. *Northern England Journal of Medicine, 285,* 201-203.

Frone, M. R., Russell, M., & Cooper, M. L. (1991). Relationship of work and family stressors to psychological distress: The independent moderating influence of social support, mastery, active coping, and self-focused attention. *Journal of Social Behavior and Personality, 6,* 227-250.

Ganster, D. C. (1987). Type A behavior and occupational stress. In J. M. Ivancevich & D. C. Ganster (Eds.), *Job stress: From theory to suggestion* (pp. 61-84). New York: Haworth.

Ganster, D. C., Fusilier, M. R., & Mayes, B. T. (1986). Role of social support in the experience of stress at work. *Journal of Applied Psychology, 71,* 102-110.

Ganster, D. C., & Schaubroeck, J. (1991a). Role stress and worker health: An extension of the plasticity hypothesis. *Journal of Social Behavior and Personality, 6,* 349-360.

Ganster, D. C., & Schaubroeck, J. (1991b). Work stress and employee health. *Journal of Management, 17,* 235-271.

George, J. M., & Bettenhausen, K. (1990). Understanding prosocial behavior, sales performance, and turnover: A group-level analysis. *Journal of Applied Psychology, 75,* 698-709.

Giles, W. F. (1977). Volunteering for job enrichment: A test of expectancy theory predictions. *Personnel Psychology, 30,* 427-435.

Goldstein, I. L. (1993). *Training in organizations* (3rd ed.). Pacific Grove, CA: Brooks/Cole.

Gore, S. (1987). Perspectives on social support and research on stress moderating processes. In J. M. Ivancevich & D. C. Ganster (Eds.), *Job stress: From theory to suggestion* (pp. 85-101). New York: Haworth.

Greenhaus, J. H., & Parasuraman, S. (1986). A work-nonwork interactive perspective of stress and its consequences. *Journal of Organizational Behavior Management, 8,* 37-60.

Griffin, R. W. (1991). Effects of work redesign on employee perceptions, attitudes, and behaviors: A longitudinal investigation. *Academy of Management Journal, 34,* 425-435.

Gupta, N., & Jenkins, D. G. (1985). Dual career couples: Stress, stressors, strains, and strategies. In T. A. Beehr & R. S. Bhagat (Eds.), *Human stress and cognition in organizations* (pp. 141-176). New York: John Wiley.

Hackman, J. R., & Oldham, G. R. (1975). Development of the Job Diagnostic Survey. *Journal of Applied Psychology, 60,* 159-170.

Hackman, J. R., & Oldham, G. R. (1980). *Work redesign.* Reading, MA: Addison-Wesley.

Hassell, B., & Perrewe, P. (1993). An examination of the relationship between older workers' perceptions of age discrimination and employee psychological states. *Journal of Managerial Issues, 5,* 109-120.

Heinisch, D. A., & Jex, S. M. (1996, April). *Self vs. observer rating: Negative affectivity's role in occupational stress.* Paper presented at the annual meeting of the Society for Industrial and Organizational Psychology, San Diego, CA.

Henry, R., & Hulin, C. L. (1987). Stability of skilled performance across time: Some generalizations and limitations on utilities. *Journal of Applied Psychology, 72,* 457-462.

Henry, R., & Hulin, C. L. (1989). Changing validities: Ability-performance relations and utilities. *Journal of Applied Psychology, 74,* 365-367.

Hillenberg, J. B., & Wolf, K. L. (1988). Psychological impact of traumatic events: Implications for employee assistance interventions. *Employee Assistance Quarterly, 4,* 1-13.

Hogan, E. A., & Overmeyer-Day, L. (1994). The psychology of mergers and acquisitions. In C. L. Cooper & I. T. Robertson (Eds.), *International review of industrial and organizational psychology 1994* (Vol. 9, pp. 247-280). Chichester, UK: Wiley.

Human capital: The decline of America's workforce. (1988, September 19). *Business Week,* pp. 100-141.

Human Capital Initiative. (1993, October). Making people and technology work together. *American Psychological Society Observer, 1,* 1-65.

Hunter, J. E., & Schmidt, F. L. (1990). *Methods of meta-analysis: Correcting error and bias in research findings.* Newbury Park, CA: Sage.

Hurrell, J. J., Jr. (1995). Commentary: Police work, occupational stress, and individual coping. *Journal of Organizational Behavior, 16,* 27-28.

Hurrell, J. J., Jr., & Colligan, M. J. (1987). Machine pacing and shiftwork: Evidence for job stress. In J. M. Ivancevich & D. C. Ganster (Eds.), *Job stress: From theory to suggestion* (pp. 159-176). New York: Haworth.

Idaszak, J. R., & Drasgow, F. (1987). A revision of the Job Diagnostic Survey: Elimination of a measurement artifact. *Journal of Applied Psychology, 72,* 69-74.

Inzana, C. M., Driskell, J. E., Salas, E., & Johnston, J. H. (1996). Effects of preparatory information on enhancing performance under stress. *Journal of Applied Psychology, 81,* 429-435.

Ivancevich, J. M. (1979). An analysis of participation in decision making among project engineers. *Academy of Management Journal, 22,* 253-269.

Ivancevich, J. M., & Matteson, M. T. (1980). *Stress and work: A managerial perspective*. Glenview, IL: Scott, Foresman.

Ivancevich, J. M., & Matteson, M. T. (1988). Type A behavior and the healthy individual. *British Journal of Medical Psychology, 61*, 37-56.

Ivancevich, J. M., Matteson, M. T., & Richards, E. P. (1985, March-April). Who's liable for stress on the job? *Harvard Business Review*, pp. 60-72.

Jackson, S. E., & Schuler, R. S. (1985). A meta-analysis and conceptual critique of research on role ambiguity and role conflict in work settings. *Organizational Behavior and Human Decision Processes, 36*, 16-78.

Jamal, M. (1984). Job stress and job performance controversy: An empirical assessment. *Organizational Behavior and Human Performance, 33*, 1-21.

Jamal, M. (1985). Relationship of job stress to job performance: A study of managers and blue collar workers. *Human Relations, 38*, 409-424.

James, L. A., & James, L. R. (1989). Integrating work environment perceptions: Explorations into the measurement of meaning. *Journal of Applied Psychology, 74*, 739-751.

Jamieson, D., & O'Mara, J. (1991). *Managing workforce 2000*. San Francisco: Jossey-Bass.

Jex, S. M. (1988). *The relationship between exercise and employee responses to work stressors: A test of two competing models*. Unpublished doctoral dissertation, University of South Florida, Tampa.

Jex, S. M., & Beehr, T. A. (1991). Emerging theoretical and methodological issues in the study of work-related stress. In G. R. Ferris & K. M. Rowland (Eds.), *Research in personnel and human resources management* (Vol. 9, pp. 311-364). Greenwich, CT: JAI.

Jex, S. M., Cvetanovski, J., & Allen, S. J. (1994). Self-esteem as a moderator of the impact of unemployment. *Journal of Social Behavior and Personality, 9*, 69-80.

Jex, S. M., & Elacqua, T. C. (in press). Self-esteem as a moderator: A comparison of global and organization-based measures. *Journal of Occupational and Organizational Psychology*.

Jex, S. M., & Gudanowski, D. M. (1992). Efficacy beliefs and work stress: An exploratory study. *Journal of Organizational Behavior, 13*, 509-517.

Jex, S. M., Hughes, P., Storr, C., Baldwin, D. C., Jr., Conard, S., & Sheehan, D. V. (1991). Behavioral consequences of job-related stress among resident physicians: The mediating role of psychological strain. *Psychological Reports, 69*, 339-349.

Jick, T. D. (1979). Mixing qualitative and quantitative methods: Triangulation in action. *Administrative Science Quarterly, 24*, 602-611.

Jick, T. D. (1985). As the ax falls: Budget cuts and the experience of stress in organizations. In T. A. Beehr & R. S. Bhagat (Eds.), *Human stress and cognition in organizations* (pp. 83-114). New York: John Wiley.

Jick, T. D., & Mitz, L. F. (1985). Sex differences in work stress. *Academy of Management Review, 10*, 408-420.

Jick, T. D., & Murray, V. V. (1982). The management of hard times: Budget cutbacks in the public sector. *Organizational Studies, 3*, 141-169.

Johns, G. (1991). Substantive and methodological constraints on behavior and attitudes in organizational research. *Organizational Behavior and Human Decision Processes, 49*, 80-104.

Johnson, J. E., & Leventhal, H. (1974). Effects of accurate expectations and behavioral instructions on reactions during a noxious medical examination. *Journal of Personality and Social Psychology, 29*, 710-718.

Johnson, P. R., & Indvik, J. (1994). Workplace violence: An issue of the nineties. *Public Personnel Management, 23*, 515-523.

Jones, B., Flynn, D. M., & Kelloway, E. K. (1995). Perception of support from the organization in relation to work stress, satisfaction, and commitment. In S. L. Sauter & L. R. Murphy (Eds.),

Organizational risk factors for job stress (pp. 41-52). Washington, DC: American Psychological Association.

Jones, J. W., Barge, B. N., Steffy, B. D., Fay, L. M., Kunz, L. K., & Wuebker, L. J. (1988). Stress and medical malpractice: Organizational risk assessment and intervention. *Journal of Applied Psychology, 73,* 727-735.

Jones, J. W., & Boye, M. W. (1992). Job stress and employee counterproductivity. In J. C. Quick, J. J. Hurrell, & L. R. Murphy (Eds.), *Stress and well-being at work* (pp. 239-251). Washington, DC: American Psychological Association.

Joyce, W. F. (1986). Matrix organization: A social experiment. *Academy of Management Journal, 29,* 536-561.

Judge, T. A., Boudreau, J. W., & Bretz, R. D., Jr. (1994). Job and life attitudes of male executives. *Journal of Applied Psychology, 79,* 767-782.

Kahn, H., & Cooper, C. L. (1990). Mental health, job satisfaction, alcohol intake and occupational stress among dealers in financial markets. *Stress Medicine, 6,* 285-298.

Kahn, R. L., & Byosiere, P. (1992). Stress in organizations. In M. D. Dunnette & L. M. Hough (Eds.), *Handbook of industrial and organizational psychology* (2nd ed., Vol. 2, pp. 571-650). Palo Alto, CA: Consulting Psychologists Press.

Kahn, R. L., Wolfe, D. M., Quinn, R. P., Snoek, J. D., & Rosenthal, R. A. (1964). *Organizational stress: Studies in role conflict and ambiguity.* New York: John Wiley.

Kahneman, D. (1973). *Attention and effort.* Englewood Cliffs, NJ: Prentice Hall.

Karasek, R. A. (1979). Job demands, job decision latitude, and mental strain: Implications for job redesign. *Administrative Science Quarterly, 24,* 285-308.

Karasek, R. A., Baker, D., Marxer, F., Ahlbom, A., & Theorell, T. (1981). Job decision latitude, job demands, and cardiovascular disease: A prospective study of Swedish men. *American Journal of Public Health, 71,* 694-705.

Katz, D., & Kahn, R. L. (1978). *The social psychology of organizations* (2nd ed.). New York: John Wiley.

Kaufmann, G. M., & Beehr, T. A. (1986). Interactions between stressors and social support: Some counterintuitive results. *Journal of Applied Psychology, 71,* 522-526.

Keenan, A., & Newton, T. J. (1985). Stressful events, stressors and psychological strains in young professional engineers. *Journal of Occupational Behavior, 6,* 151-156.

Kelloway, E. K., & Barling, J. (1990). Item content versus item wording: Disentangling role conflict and role ambiguity. *Journal of Applied Psychology, 75,* 738-742.

King, L. A., & King, D. W. (1990). Role conflict and role ambiguity: A critical assessment of construct validity. *Psychological Bulletin, 107,* 48-64.

King, R. W., & Pave, I. (1985, October 14). Stress claims are making business jumpy: All but nine states now pay compensation for job-related emotional problems. *Business Week,* pp. 152, 154.

Kinicki, A. J., & Latack, J. C. (1990). Explication of the construct of coping with involuntary job loss. *Journal of Vocational Behavior, 36,* 339-360.

Kjellberg, A. (1977). Sleep deprivation and some aspects of performance: II. Lapses and other attentional effects. *Waking and Sleeping, 1,* 145-148.

Klein, K. J., Dansereau, F., & Hall, R. J. (1994). Levels issues in theory development, data collection, and analysis. *Academy of Management Review, 19,* 195-229.

Koch, J. L., Tung, R., Gmelch, W., & Swent, B. (1982). Job stress among school administrators: Factorial dimensions and differential effects. *Journal of Applied Psychology, 67,* 493-499.

Kottage, B. E. (1992, August). Stress in the workplace. *American Society of Safety Engineers,* pp. 24-26.

Kozlowski, S. W. J., Chao, G. T., Smith, E. M., & Hedlund, J. (1993). Organizational downsizing: Strategies, interventions, and research implications. In C. L. Cooper & I. T. Robertson (Eds.), *International review of industrial and organizational psychology* (Vol. 8, pp. 263-332). London: Wiley.

Kristof, A. L. (1996). Person-organization fit: An integrative review of its conceptualizations, measurement, and implications. *Personnel Psychology, 49,* 1-49.

Kruse, B. G. (1995). *Affective and cognitive mediation of the relationship between situational constraints and organizational citizenship behaviors.* Unpublished master's thesis, Central Michigan University.

Kuhn, R. (1988). Psychological tests reduce counterproductive acts by employees. *Assets Protection, 9,* 9-12.

Landy, F. J., & Farr, J. L. (1980). Performance rating. *Psychological Bulletin, 87,* 72-107.

Landy, F. J., & Guion, R. M. (1970). Development of scales for the measurement of work motivation. *Organizational Behavior and Human Performance, 5,* 93-108.

Lawler, E. E., III. (1986). *High involvement management: Participative strategies for improving organizational performance.* San Francisco: Jossey-Bass.

Lee, C. (1992). The relation of personality and cognitive styles with job and class performance. *Journal of Organizational Behavior, 13,* 175-185.

Lee, C., Ashford, S. J., & Bobko, P. (1990). Interactive effects of "Type A" behavior and perceived control on worker performance, job satisfaction, and somatic complaints. *Academy of Management Journal, 33,* 870-881.

Lee, C., Ashford, S. J., & Jamieson, L. F. (1993). The effects of Type A dimensions and optimism on coping strategy, health, and performance. *Journal of Organizational Behavior, 14,* 143-157.

Levine, E. L. (1983). *Everything you always wanted to know about job analysis.* Tampa, FL: Mariner.

Lodahl, T. M., & Kejner, M. (1965). The definition and measurement of job involvement. *Journal of Applied Psychology, 49,* 24-33.

London House. (1980). *The Employee Attitude Inventory.* Park Ridge, IL: Author.

Lowin, A. (1968). Participative decision making: A model, literature critique, and prescriptions for research. *Organizational Behavior and Human Performance, 3,* 68-106.

Mabe, P. A., III, & West, S. G. (1982). Validity of self-evaluation of ability: A review and meta-analysis. *Journal of Applied Psychology, 67,* 280-296.

Marcus, E. H. (1988, June). Mental disability claims: A new epidemic? *CPCU Journal,* pp. 112-116.

Marcus, E. H. (1991, April). Coping with job stress claims. *Defense Counsel Journal,* pp. 250-253.

Mathieu, J. E., & Zajac, D. M. (1990). A review and meta-analysis of the antecedents, correlates, and consequences of organizational commitment. *Psychological Bulletin, 108,* 171-194.

Matteson, M. T., & Ivancevich, J. M. (1987). *Controlling work stress.* San Francisco: Jossey-Bass.

McGrath, J. E. (1976). Stress and behavior in organizations. In M. D. Dunnette (Ed.), *Handbook of industrial and organizational psychology* (pp. 1351-1395). Chicago: Rand McNally.

McGrath, J. E., & Beehr, T. A. (1990). Some temporal issues in the conceptualization and measurement of stress. *Stress Medicine, 6,* 93-104.

Meeks, S. M. (1984, September). Workers' compensation and stress. *CPCU Journal,* pp. 171-177.

Meyer, J. P., & Allen, N. J. (1997). *Commitment in the workplace: Theory, research, and application.* Thousand Oaks, CA: Sage.

Michaels, R. E., & Dixon, A. L. (1994). Sellers and buyers on the boundary: Potential moderators of role stress-job outcome relationships. *Journal of the Academy of Marketing Science, 22,* 62-73.

Mone, M. A., Mueller, G. C., & Mauland, W. (1996). The perceptions and usage of statistical power in applied psychology and management research. *Personnel Psychology, 49,* 103-120.

Moorhead, G., & Griffin, R. W. (1995). *Organizational behavior: Managing people and organizations* (4th ed.). Boston: Houghton Mifflin.

Moran, S. K., Wolff, S. C., & Green, J. E. (1995). Workers' compensation and occupational stress: Gaining control. In L. R. Murphy, J. J. Hurrell, Jr., & G. P. Keita (Eds.), *Job stress interventions* (pp. 355-368). Washington, DC: American Psychological Association.

Mossholder, K. W., Bedeian, A. G., & Armenakis, A. A. (1981). Role perceptions, satisfaction, and performance: Moderating effects of self-esteem and organizational level. *Organizational Behavior and Human Performance, 28,* 224-234.

Mossholder, K. W., Bedeian, A. G., & Armenakis, A. A. (1982). Group process-work outcome relationships: A note on the moderating impact of self-esteem. *Academy of Management Journal, 25,* 575-585.

Motowidlo, S. J., Packard, J. S., & Manning, M. R. (1986). Occupational stress: Its causes and consequences for job performance. *Journal of Applied Psychology, 71,* 618-629.

Mount, M. K., & Barrick, M. R. (1995). The Big Five personality dimensions: Implications for research and practice in human resources management. In G. R. Ferris (Ed.), *Research in personnel and human resources management* (Vol. 13, pp. 153-200). Greenwich, CT: JAI.

Mowday, R. T., Steers, R. M., & Porter, L. W. (1979). The measurement of organizational commitment. *Journal of Vocational Behavior, 14,* 224-247.

Muchinsky, P. M. (1993). *Psychology applied to work* (4th ed.). Pacific Grove, CA: Brooks/Cole.

Mulcahy, C. (1991, May 20). Workplace stress reaches "epidemic" proportion. *National Underwriter,* pp. 4, 20.

Murphy, K. R. (1986). When your top choice turns you down: Effect of rejected offers on the utility of selection tests. *Psychological Bulletin, 99,* 133-138.

Murphy, K. R. (1989). Dimensions of job performance. In R. Dillion & J. W. Pellegrino (Eds.), *Testing: Theoretical and applied perspectives* (pp. 218-247). New York: Praeger.

Murphy, K. R. (1990). Job performance and productivity. In K. R. Murphy & F. J. Saal (Eds.), *Psychology in organizations: Integrating science and practice* (pp. 157-176). Hillsdale, NJ: Lawrence Erlbaum.

Murphy, K. R. (1994). Toward a broader conception of jobs and job performance: Impact of changes in the military environment on the structure, assessment, and prediction of job performance. In M. G. Rumsey, C. B. Walker, & J. H. Harris (Eds.), *Personnel selection and classification* (pp. 85-102). Hillsdale, NJ: Lawrence Erlbaum.

Murphy, K. R., & Cleveland, J. N. (1990). *Performance appraisal: An organizational perspective.* Boston: Allyn & Bacon.

Murphy, S. A., Beaton, R. D., Cain, K., & Pike, K. (1994). Gender differences in firefighter job stressors and symptoms of stress. *Women & Health, 22,* 55-69.

National Council on Compensation Insurance. (1988). *Emotional stress in the workplace: New legal rights in the eighties.* New York: Author.

National Council on Compensation Insurance. (1991). *Issues report, 1991.* Boca Raton, FL: Author.

Netemeyer, R., Johnston, M., & Burton, S. (1990). Analysis of role conflict and role ambiguity in a structural equations framework. *Journal of Applied Psychology, 75,* 148-157.

Nowack, K. M., & Hanson, A. L. (1983, November). The relationship between stress, job performance, and burnout in college student resident assistants. *Journal of College Student Personnel,* 545-550.

Nunnally, J. C., & Bernstein, I. H. (1994). *Psychometric theory* (3rd ed.). New York: McGraw-Hill.

O'Connor, E. J., Peters, L. H., Eulberg, J. R., & Watson, T. W. (1984, August). *Situational constraints in Air Force work settings: Effects on performance, affective reactions and reenlistment plans.* Paper presented at the annual meeting of the Academy of Management, Boston.

O'Connor, E. J., Peters, L. H., Pooyan, A., Weekley, J., Frank, B., & Erenkrantz, B. (1984). Situational constraint effects on performance, affective reactions and turnover: A field replication and extension. *Journal of Applied Psychology, 69,* 663-672.

O'Connor, E. J., Peters, L. H., & Segovis, J. C. (1983). Situational constraints, task relevant abilities, and experienced frustration. *Personnel Selection and Training Bulletin, 4,* 178-188.

O'Donnell, M. L., & Krumreich, T. A. (1989, September-October). Employer's liability for job stress continues to increase. *Journal of Compensation and Benefits,* 85-91.

Ones, D. S., Viswesvaran, C., & Schmidt, F. L. (1993). Comprehensive meta-analysis of integrity test validities: Findings and implications for personnel selection and theories of performance. *Journal of Applied Psychology, 78,* 679-703.

O'Reilly, C. A., Chatman, J., & Caldwell, D. F. (1991). People and organizational culture: A profile comparison approach to assessing person-organization fit. *Academy of Management Journal, 34,* 487-516.

Organ, D. W. (1977). A reappraisal and reinterpretation of the satisfaction-causes-performance hypothesis. *Academy of Management Review, 2,* 46-53.

Organ, D. W. (1994). Organizational citizenship behavior and the good soldier. In M. G. Rumsey, C. B. Walker, & J. H. Harris (Eds.), *Personnel selection and classification* (pp. 53-67). Hillsdale, NJ: Lawrence Erlbaum.

Organ, D. W., & Ryan, K. (1995). A meta-analytic review of attitudinal and dispositional predictors of organizational citizenship behavior. *Personnel Psychology, 48,* 775-802.

Orpen, C. (1982). The effect of social support on reactions to role ambiguity and role conflict: A study among white and black clerks in South Africa. *Journal of Cross-Cultural Psychology, 13,* 375-384.

Ostroff, C. (1992). The relationship between satisfaction, attitudes, and performance: An organizational-level analysis. *Journal of Applied Psychology, 77,* 963-974.

Parker, P. A., & Kulik, J. A. (1995). Burnout, self- and supervisor-rated job performance, and absenteeism among nurses. *Journal of Behavioral Medicine, 18,* 581-599.

Payne, R. (1991). Individual differences in cognition and the stress process. In C. L. Cooper & R. Payne (Eds.), *Personality and stress: Individual differences in the stress process* (pp. 181-204). New York: John Wiley.

Payne, R. L., Jabri, M. M., & Pearson, A. W. (1988). On the importance of knowing the affective meaning of job demands. *Journal of Organizational Behavior, 9,* 149-158.

Perrewe, P. L., & Ganster, D. C. (1989). The impact of job demands and behavioral control on experienced job stress. *Journal of Organizational Behavior, 10,* 213-229.

Peters, L. H., Fisher, C. D., & O'Connor, E. J. (1982). The moderating effect of situational control of performance variance on the relationship between individual differences and performance. *Personnel Psychology, 35,* 609-621.

Peters, L. H., & O'Connor, E. J. (1980). Situational constraints and work outcomes: The influences of a frequently overlooked construct. *Academy of Management Review, 5,* 391-397.

Peters, L. H., & O'Connor, E. J. (1988). Measuring work obstacles: Procedures, issues, and implications. In F. D. Schoorman & B. Schneider (Eds.), *Facilitating work effectiveness* (pp. 105-123). Lexington, MA: Lexington Books.

Peters, L. H., O'Connor, E. J., & Rudolf, C. J. (1980). The behavioral and affective consequences of performance-relevant situational variables. *Organizational Behavior and Human Performance, 25,* 79-96.

Pierce, J. L., Gardner, D. G., Cummings, L. L., & Dunham, R. B. (1989). Organization-based self-esteem: Construct definition, measurement, and validation. *Academy of Management Journal, 32,* 622-648.

Pierce, J. L., Gardner, D. G., Dunham, R. B., & Cummings, L. L. (1993). Moderation by organization-based self-esteem on role condition-employee response relationships. *Academy of Management Journal, 36,* 271-288.

Poulton, E., Hunt, G., Carpenter, A. L., & Edwards, R. (1978). The performance of junior doctors following reduced sleep and long hours of work. *Ergonomics, 21,* 279-295.

Pritchard, R. D. (1992). Organizational productivity. In M. D. Dunnette & L. M. Hough (Eds.), *Handbook of industrial and organizational psychology* (2nd ed., Vol. 3, pp. 443-471). Palo Alto, CA: Consulting Psychologists Press.

Pulakos, E. D. (1984). A comparison of rater training programs: Error training and accuracy training. *Journal of Applied Psychology, 69,* 581-588.

Quinones, M. A., Ford, J. K., & Teachout, M. S. (1995). The relationship between work experience and job performance: A conceptual and meta-analytic review. *Personnel Psychology, 48,* 887-910.

Rechtschaffen, A., & Kales, A. (1968). *Manual of standardized terminology techniques and scoring system for sleep stages in human subjects.* Washington, DC: Government Printing Office.

Rizzo, J. R., House, R. J., & Lirtzman, S. I. (1970). Role conflict and ambiguity in complex organizations. *Administrative Science Quarterly, 15,* 150-163.

Roberts, C. K. (1995). *The role of personality in perceived free riding.* Unpublished doctoral dissertation, Central Michigan University.

Rosenthal, R. (1991). *Meta-analytic techniques for social research* (Rev. ed.). Newbury Park, CA: Sage.

Rotter, J. (1966). Generalized expectancies for internal versus external control of reinforcement. *Psychological Monographs, 80* (entire issue, No. 609).

Rubin, B. L. (1991, January). Europeans value diversity. *HR Magazine,* pp. 38-41, 78.

Runyon, K. E. (1973). Some interactions between personality variables and management styles. *Journal of Applied Psychology, 57,* 288-294.

Ryan, A. M., Schmit, M. J., & Johnson, R. (1996). Attitudes and effectiveness: Examining relations at an organizational level. *Personnel Psychology, 49,* 853-882.

Sagie, A. (1995). Employee participation and work outcomes. *Academy of Management Review, 20,* 278-280.

Salvendy, G. (1972). Physiological and psychological aspects of paced and unpaced performance. *Acta Physiologica, 42,* 267-275.

Sauter, S. L., Murphy, L. M., & Hurrell, J. J., Jr. (1990). Prevention of work-related psychological disorders. *American Psychologist, 45,* 1146-1158.

Schaubroeck, J., Ganster, D. C., Sime, W. E., & Ditman, D. (1993). A field experiment testing supervisory role clarification. *Personnel Psychology, 46,* 1-25.

Schein, E. H. (1978). *Career dynamics: Matching individual and organizational needs.* Reading, MA: Addison-Wesley.

Schmidt, F. L., & Hunter, J. E. (1978). Moderator research and the law of small numbers. *Personnel Psychology, 31,* 215-232.

Schuler, R. S. (1975). Role perceptions, satisfaction and performance: A partial reconciliation. *Journal of Applied Psychology, 60,* 683-687.

Schuler, R. S. (1977). The effects of role perceptions on employee satisfaction and performance moderated by employee ability. *Organizational Behavior and Human Performance, 18,* 98-117.

Schultz, D., & Schultz, S. E. (1998). *Psychology and work today: An introduction to industrial and organizational psychology* (7th ed.). Englewood Cliffs, NJ: Prentice Hall.

Seligman, M. E. P. (1975). *Helplessness: On depression, development, and death.* San Francisco: Freeman.

Selye, H. (1956). *The stress of life.* New York: McGraw-Hill.

Shalowitz, D. (1991, May 20). Another health care headache: Job stress could strain corporate budgets: Study. *Business Insurance,* pp. 3, 21-22.

Sharit, J., & Czaja, S. J. (1994). Aging, computer-based task performance, and stress: Issues and challenges. *Ergonomics, 37,* 559-577.

Sheridan, P. J. (1987, May). Workplace stress spurs costly claims. *Occupational Hazards,* pp. 81-84.

Smith, C. S., Tisak, J., & Schmieder, R. A. (1993). The measurement properties of the role conflict and role ambiguity scales: A review and extension of the empirical research. *Journal of Organizational Behavior, 14,* 37-48.

Sparks, K., Cooper, C., Fried, Y., & Shirom, A. (1997). The effect of hours of work on health: A meta-analytic review. *Journal of Occupational and Organizational Psychology, 70,* 391-408.

Spector, P. E. (1982). Behavior in organizations as a function of employee locus of control. *Psychological Bulletin, 91,* 482-497.

Spector, P. E. (1986). Perceived control by employees: A meta-analysis of studies concerning autonomy and participation at work. *Human Relations, 39,* 1005-1016.

Spector, P. E. (1987). Interactive effects of perceived control and job stressors on affective reactions and health outcomes for clerical workers. *Work & Stress, 1,* 155-162.

Spector, P. E. (1992). A consideration of the validity and meaning of self-report measures of job conditions. In C. L. Cooper & I. T. Robertson (Eds.), *International review of industrial and organizational psychology 1992* (pp. 123-151). Chichester, UK: Wiley.

Spector, P. E. (1994). Using self-report questionnaires in OB research: A comment on the use of a controversial method. *Journal of Organizational Behavior, 15,* 385-392.

Spector, P. E. (1996). *Industrial and organizational psychology: Research and practice.* New York: John Wiley.

Spector, P. E. (1997a). *Job satisfaction: Application, assessment, causes, and consequences.* Thousand Oaks, CA: Sage.

Spector, P. E. (1997b). The role of frustration in anti-social behavior at work. In R. A. Giacalone & J. Greenberg (Eds.), *Anti-social behavior in the workplace* (pp. 1-17). Thousand Oaks, CA: Sage.

Spector, P. E., Dwyer, D. J., & Jex, S. M. (1988). Relation of job stressors to affective, health, and performance outcomes: A comparison of multiple data sources. *Journal of Applied Psychology, 73,* 11-19.

Spector, P. E., & Jex, S. M. (1991). Relations of job characteristics from multiple data sources with employee affect, absence, turnover intentions, and health. *Journal of Applied Psychology, 76,* 46-53.

Spector, P. E., Jex, S. M., & Chen, P. Y. (1995). Personality traits as predictors of job characteristics. *Journal of Organizational Behavior, 16,* 59-65.

Spector, P. E., & O'Connell, B. J. (1994). The contribution of individual dispositions to the subsequent perceptions of job stressors and job strains. *Journal of Occupational and Organizational Psychology, 67,* 1-11.

Spence, J. T., Helmreich, R. L., & Pred, R. S. (1987). Impatience versus achievement strivings in the Type A pattern: Differential effects on students' health and academic achievement. *Journal of Applied Psychology, 72,* 522-528.

Spielberger, C. D., & Reheiser, E. C. (1994). The Job Stress Survey: Measuring gender differences in occupational stress. *Journal of Social Behavior and Personality, 9,* 199-218.

Spurgeon, A., & Harrington, J. M. (1989). Work performance and health of junior hospital doctors: A review of the literature. *Work & Stress, 3,* 117-128.

Steel, R. P., & Mento, A. J. (1986). Impact of situational constraints on subjective and objective criteria of managerial job performance. *Organizational Behavior and Human Decision Processes, 37,* 254-265.

Steel, R. P., & Mento, A. J. (1987). The participation-performance controversy reconsidered. *Group and Organization Studies, 12,* 411-423.

Sternberg, R. J. (1985). *Beyond IQ: A triarchic theory of human intelligence.* New York: Cambridge University Press.

Sternberg, R. J. (1994). The PRSVL model of person-context interaction in the study of human potential. In M. G. Rumsey, C. B. Walker, & J. H. Harris (Eds.), *Personnel selection and classification* (pp. 317-332). Hillsdale, NJ: Lawrence Erlbaum.

Storms, P. L., & Spector, P. E. (1987). Relationships of organizational frustration with reported behavioral reactions: The moderating effect of locus of control. *Journal of Occupational Psychology, 60,* 227-234.

Suarez, E. C., & Williams, R. B. (1990). The relationship between dimensions of hostility and cardiovascular reactivity as a function of task characteristics. *Psychosomatic Medicine, 52,* 558-570.

Sullivan, S. E., & Bhagat, R. S. (1992). Organizational stress, job satisfaction, and job performance: Where do we go from here? *Journal of Management, 18,* 353-374.

Swap, W. C., & Rubin, J. Z. (1983). Measurement of interpersonal orientation. *Journal of Personality and Social Psychology, 44,* 208-219.

Thurstone, L. L. (1953). *Thurstone Temperament Schedule.* Chicago: Science Research Associates.

Tracey, J. B., Tannenbaum, S. I., & Kavanagh, M. J. (1995). Applying trained skills on the job: The importance of the work environment. *Journal of Applied Psychology, 80,* 239-252.

Tracy, L., & Johnson, T. W. (1981). What do the role conflict and role ambiguity scales measure? *Journal of Applied Psychology, 66,* 464-469.

Tubre, T. C., Sifferman, J. J., & Collins, J. M. (1996, April). *Jackson and Schuler (1985) revisited: A meta-analytic review of the relationship between role stress and job performance.* Paper presented at the annual meeting of the Society for Industrial and Organizational Psychology, San Diego, CA.

Turnage, J. J., & Spielberger, C. D. (1991). Job stress in managers, professionals, and clerical workers. *Work & Stress, 5,* 165-176.

Villanova, P. (1996). Predictive validity of situational constraints in general versus specific performance domains. *Journal of Applied Psychology, 81,* 532-547.

Villanova, P., Bernardin, H. J., Johnson, D. L., & Dahmus, S. A. (1994). The validity of a measure of job compatibility in the prediction of job performance and turnover of motion picture theater personnel. *Personnel Psychology, 47,* 73-90.

Viswesvaran, C., Ones, D. S., & Schmidt, F. L. (1996). Comparative analysis of the reliability of performance ratings. *Journal of Applied Psychology, 81,* 557-574..

Wagner, J. A. (1994). Participation's effect on performance and satisfaction: A reconsideration of research evidence. *Academy of Management Review, 19,* 312-330.

Wagner, J. A., & Gooding, R. Z. (1987). Shared influence and organizational behavior: A meta-analysis of situational variables expected to moderate participation-outcome relationships. *Academy of Management Journal, 30,* 524-541.

Wanous, J., & Colella, A. (1989). Organizational entry research: Current status and future directions. In K. M. Rowland & G. R. Ferris (Eds.), *Research in personnel and human resources management* (Vol. 7, pp. 59-120). Greenwich, CT: JAI.

Webb, W. B., & Levy, C. H. (1984). Effects of spaced and repeated sleep deprivation. *Ergonomics, 27,* 45-58.

Xie, J. L., & Johns, G. (1995). Job scope and stress: Can scope be too high? *Academy of Management Journal, 38,* 1288-1309.

Yerkes, R. M., & Dodson, J. D. (1908). The relation of strength of stimulus to rapidity of habit formation. *Journal of Comparative Neurological Psychology, 18,* 459-482.

Yukl, G. (1992). Theory and research on leadership in organizations. In M. D. Dunnette & L. M. Hough (Eds.), *Handbook of industrial and organizational psychology* (2nd ed., Vol. 3, pp. 147-198). Palo Alto, CA: Consulting Psychologists Press.

Index